APATHETIC CHRISTIANITY
THE ZOMBIE RELIGION OF AMERICAN CHURCHIANITY
IT WILL FEEL YOUR NEEDS AND FEED YOUR FLESH

WWW.R3VOLUTION PRESS.COM

> WHAT DOES IT PROFIT A MAN TO HAVE HIS BEST LIFE NOW AND LOSE HIS ETERNAL SOUL?
>
> WHAT DOES IT PROFIT THE CHURCH TO GAIN FAVOR WITH THE WORLD AND LOSE HER ETERNAL COMMISSION?

APATHETIC CHRISTIANITY
THE ZOMBIE RELIGION OF AMERICAN CHURCHIANITY

IT WILL FEEL YOUR NEEDS AND FEED YOUR FLESH

BY SCOTT ALAN BUSS

www.FIREBREATHINGCHRISTIAN.com

APATHETIC CHRISTIANITY: The Zombie Religion of American Churchianity, Volume 1
4th Edition

Copyright © 2011, 2012, 2015 Scott Alan Buss

All rights reserved. No part of this book may be reproduced in any form or by any means, electronic, mechanical, photocopying, scanning, or otherwise, without permission in writing from the author, except by a reviewer who may quote brief passages in a review.

Published by:
R3VOLUTION PRESS
Chapel Hill, TN

Jacket and interior designs by Scott Alan Buss

All Bible verses, unless otherwise noted, are taken from the *English Standard Version* (Copyright © 2001 and used by permission of Crossway Bibles, a division of Good News Publishers).

Also quoted:
The New King James Version
Copyright © 1979,1980,1982. Used by permission of Thomas Nelson, Inc. All rights reserved.

The New Living Translation
Copyright © 1996, 2004. Used by permission of Tyndale House Publishers, Inc. All rights reserved.

R3VOLUTION PRESS Books are available at special discounts for bulk purchases. R3VOLUTION PRESS also publishes books in electronic formats. For more information, please visit www.R3VOLUTIONPRESS.com or www.ApatheticChristianity.com.

ISBN 13 Digit: 978-0-9838122-5-8
Printed in the United States of America

For Trina and Jan—

two Fire Breathing Sisters, without whom this work and mission would not have been possible…by His grace and for His glory.

CONTENTS

INTRODUCTION: LIGHT AND GRACE IN THE LAND OF THE DEAD — 1
OUR SUPERNATURAL WAR ON ZOMBIE RELIGION

SECTION 1: THE ZOMBIE RELIGION OF AMERICAN CHURCHIANITY

CHAPTER 1: PASTOR FEELGOOD AND HIS ALL-AMERICAN SALVATION MACHINE — 21
HE WILL FEEL YOUR NEEDS AND FEED YOUR FLESH

CHAPTER 2: THE PROBLEM WITH DEAD PEOPLE — 43
THE FUTILITY OF ZOMBIE HERDING

CHAPTER 3: FLU SHOT JESUS: CANDY CHRISTIANITY'S MAGICAL SUPERPAL — 55
AMERICA'S FAVORITE ANTI-CHRIST

CHAPTER 4: McGOSPEL SALVATION: SO LIFELESS A DEAD MAN CAN DO IT — 69
THE STICKY SWEET POISON OF EASY BELIEVISM

SECTION 2: THE FLESH-DRIVEN CHURCH OF THE LIVING DEAD

CHAPTER 5: HOWLING WOLVES, BLOATED GOATS, AND STARVING SHEEP — 83
McGOSPEL TRUTHS AND CONSEQUENCES

CHAPTER 6: SIX FLAGS OVER JESUS — 99
THE MALL OF AMERICAN CHURCHIANITY

CHAPTER 7: THE CORROSIVE CHARACTER OF CANDY CHRISTIANITY — 109
THE ANTI-CHRISTIAN PRODUCT OF AN ANTI-CHRISTIAN GOSPEL

SECTION 3: THE RAZING OF HELL

CHAPTER 8: RAISING THE DEAD — 125
THE SUPERNATURAL POWER OF THE SUPERNATURAL GOSPEL

CHAPTER 9: RAZING HELL — 141
TAKING THE TRUTH WAR TO ZOMBIELAND

CHAPTER 10: RAISING HIS BANNER — 157
THE SALVATION OF A NATION - ONE ZOMBIE AT A TIME

AFTERGLOW: FOR THE LOVE OF THE KING — 171
THE DEFINING MISSION OF THE COMMON BELIEVER

ACKNOWLEDGMENTS — 183

ABOUT THE AUTHOR — 185

LIGHT AND GRACE IN THE LAND OF THE DEAD

OUR SUPERNATURAL WAR ON ZOMBIE RELIGION

AN INTRODUCTION

LIGHT AND GRACE IN THE LAND OF THE DEAD

"I don't read the Bible very much, and I really don't want to." She spoke calmly and clearly, sitting there as we talked over the kitchen table the way we had a hundred times before. Then, between sips from a favorite black coffee cup, she almost casually elaborated, "And I don't feel bad about it at all. I really don't."

I say "almost casually" because she was clearly charting a course methodically and with purpose, yet there was also a certain nonchalant, matter-of-fact coolness to her delivery that either was cover for a deeper struggle that she wished to avoid, or an honest representation of the position to which she had resigned herself on the matter. I couldn't tell which.

Her contentedness seemed to grow with every passing syllable. This was accompanied by a quickening of pace, as though there was something important waiting on the other side of her presentation.

"I know I'm supposed to [feel bad], but I don't. I know that [the Bible] says to do certain things that I don't do, but I don't want to do those things and I don't plan to do them, to be honest. I'm fine with that, really."

By now she was beyond calm and well into a silky smooth autopilot mode. She had the confidence of the fit, self-aware, forty-something career-minded woman that she was.

"I don't care if I just barely make it in; I'm just glad to be going to Heaven."

And there it was: The Point.

"That's all I want. I just want to go to Heaven."

INTRODUCTION

I can remember those few sentences as if they were spoken to me only yesterday, though now many years have passed since that particular moment with that particular woman in that particular kitchen. Then, as now, I was struck by her ever-so-freely offered words, though time has brought increased clarity – and increased alarm – over their meaning.

She was not doing and had no interest in doing what she already knew the Bible had to say about this, that, or the other thing, and she certainly didn't have any desire to learn more about what it might say about the *other* other things she hadn't already accidentally discovered, but she was happy, confident and oh-so- comfortable in the embrace of the soothing notion that she was, in fact, at the end of the day – or at the end of her days, Heaven bound.

If there was one thing that she knew about eternity – her eternity, it was that she was securely saved and going to that beautiful place.

Her pastor told her so.

Her church told her so.

Her friends told her so.

Practically everyone in her Bible Belt American culture told her so.

And they all go on telling her so. Seven days a week and twice on Sundays.

This is the primary mission and consequence of the dominant religion of post-Christian America, which also just happens to be the religion that spearheaded the inauguration of America's post-Christian era.

Its god isn't angry at anyone. He's far too nice for that; a whole lot more like Santa Claus than Yahweh, to be sure.

Its gospel isn't a command to repent and turn from sin so that one might avoid the coming righteous judgment of a holy, distinctly un-Santa-like God. It's more of a pleading request from a weak, undemanding wannabe messiah/therapist who is just begging you to get out of the line going to hell (if there really even is such a place) and get into the line going to heaven, so that you might instantly and permanently qualify for his no-strings-attached, super-sized plan for your best life now.

With that god and that gospel, this religion's members are just what you'd naturally expect: Millions upon millions of content and confident, flesh-obsessed walking dead who think like the world, act like the world, love what the world loves and hate what the world hates…all in Jesus' name.

It's that last bit – the "in Jesus' name" part – that really does make all of the difference here. It's the spark that has ignited the engine. It is through His name that credibility has been attained, ministries have been founded, and empires have been built, and it is through the abuse of His name, nature, Word, and Gospel, that this credibility, these ministries, and these empires have been empowered to twist and hold those who profess Him as Savior into a position of direct opposition to Him as Lord.

In His name, we have been called to abandon good and righteous judgment.

In His name, we've been called to make man's happiness the center of all things, including religion.

In His name, we've been called to tolerate and even love the things that He hates.

In His name, we have been called to "be nicer" than…Him.

In His name, we have witnessed the construction of the very machinery now used to most effectively malign His holy name, openly mock His perfect truth, and wage war on His chosen people.

Welcome to American Churchianity.

INTRODUCTION

THE CHURCH OF THE LIVING DEAD

See to it that no one takes you captive by philosophy and empty deceit, according to human tradition, according to the elemental spirits of the world, and not according to Christ.

Colossians 2:8

For the time is coming when people will not endure sound teaching, but having itching ears they will accumulate for themselves teachers to suit their own passions, and will turn away from listening to the truth and wander off into myths.

2 Timothy 4:3-4

While George Romero's *Night of the Living Dead* is widely credited with the inauguration of the modern zombie concept, a strong case can be made for none other than God the Spirit through His perfect written Word as the original author of zombie mythos. After all, it is His hand that wrote of the true nature of fallen man in such startlingly vivid, much-better-than-Technicolor detail, that many who read it simply cannot endure prolonged exposure to the picture that it paints. They recoil and they resist. They object and they protest. Such is the horror of fallen man's reality.

Scripture paints a picture of fallen men and women in this real world that is far bleaker than the shambling hordes of "living dead" that dot the landscapes imagined by the likes of George Romero. It's not even close, really.

Consider for yourself the following truths concerning fallen men and women as revealed in Scripture:
- Fallen men and women are spiritually dead. Not spiritually "wounded" or spiritually "hobbled" or spiritually "critical", but spiritually *dead*.
- Fallen men and women, though spiritually dead, are physically animated for a time. Thus, they walk and wander the countryside, so to speak, doing whatever appeals to their spiritually dead, flesh-obsessed nature.
- Fallen men and women love the flesh. It is what inspires them and what they constantly strive to feed and feed upon.
- Fallen men and women have a burning passion to gnaw, maul, and generally obliterate all that is truly holy and good – particularly the spiritually living.
- Fallen men and women, while they shamble about and seek to fulfill their (fallen) natural desires, have absolutely no awareness of a higher world or calling of any sort. They only see what their dead nature allows them to see. They are bound and their wills are defined by this dead nature, and they act accordingly.
- Fallen men and women can do nothing to save themselves from this state. They…are…dead.

Where the biblical account of zombie nature deviates from the more contemporary Romero spin on the concept is that one of the greatest longings and habits of actual zombies is for the formation and promotion of religion.

Zombie religion.

And it is here where one of the brightest, boldest, and most important battle lines is drawn.

INTRODUCTION

On one side are zombies. They are completely dead spiritually, self-obsessed slaves to sin, lovers of the flesh, and haters of holiness and its Author.

On the other side are supernaturally regenerated "new creatures" in Christ. They are slaves to Christ, Gospel-fueled, lovers of the Lord and His truth. They are called and empowered to wage war against all that would stand in opposition to Him.

It is important to note that everyone is a member of one group or the other, and that every member of Group B was once a member of Group A. In other words, every single member of "Team New Creature" was once an obliviously content, spiritually dead and doomed member of "Team Zombie"...until the hand of God intervened, moving them out from one camp and into the other.

The one and only determining difference between the zombie and the new creature is the grace of God. This truth, when held closely, will be of great assistance as we consider the subject of zombie evangelism.

ON GRACE AND ZOMBIES

For who regards you as superior? What do you have that you did not receive? And if you did receive it, why do you boast as if you had not received it?

1 Corinthians 4:7 (NASB)

One goal of this book is to inspire righteous anger.

The anger part of that "righteous anger" formula is all too easy to find and foment. It comes quite quickly and easily to us by nature. It's the righteous part of the equation that's often a profound challenge in light of that very same nature, but this is a challenge that we, as new creatures in Christ, are commanded and equipped to overcome. With that in mind, this seems like a perfect time to remind ourselves that, as even the zombies so often like to say: "There, but by the grace of God, go I."

This is true. Totally true. Even when a zombie says it.

And this truth means that, among other things, you and I both were once flesh-loving, God-hating zombies, right up until the very moment that He chose to save us. Let that soak some, even if you already have a solid understanding of this truth.

You and I once hated God by our spiritually dead nature, and we loved sin by the same. We once sat squarely positioned under the soon-coming righteous judgment of that same holy God and were incapable of moving – or even *desiring* to move – off that mark by even a single solitary millimeter. We loved it there because we hated Him. We loved what He hates and hated what He loves. We were that dead, or what we call 'round these parts: "a zombie". I was a zombie. You were a zombie.

INTRODUCTION

And it was in this putrid, sin-loving, truth-despising, God-hating state that He found and saved you, bringing you from death to life and infusing you with a new nature that inspired you to love the things you once hated and hate the things you once loved. He did this for you while you hated Him.

How's that hit your sense of personal superiority…or even your sense of an autonomous ability to do anything good at all?

Pretty hard, I hope.

Only with our self-esteem properly obliterated are we able to even enter the arena of battle known as "evangelism" with any real sense of coherence and credibility – precisely because we must realize that *all* of the credibility is of Him and none of it is of us – even when it comes to the subject of our own supernatural conversion. Everything that we have or know – every thought, impulse, desire, hope, dream, accomplishment or bit of progress in any area of life – is all a gift from Him to us. We have no claim to personal glory here. And only in embracing this truth are we properly equipped to "wage the good warfare" and "fight the good fight" where this modern day American Churchianity-fueled zombie apocalypse is concerned.

This total, perfect grace permeates and defines the only supernatural message with the power to bring true life to the walking dead. And we are called to bring that message – and that life – to those zombies.

THEIR SLAVERY, OUR SLAVERY, AND THE NOTHING IN-BETWEEN

> *But thanks be to God, that **you who were once slaves of sin** have become obedient from the heart to the standard of teaching to which you were committed, and, **having been set free from sin, have become slaves of righteousness**.*
>
> Romans 6:17-18 (Bold emphasis added)

As we progress through the subjects covered here and in future volumes, the fact that all are slaves – either slaves to sin or slaves to Christ – should remain in the forefront of our consciousness, etched prayerfully into a position of prominence so that we might better accomplish the very challenging goal of balancing three vital – and challenging – aspects of the Christian walk:

1. **Personal Humility** – We were zombies when He bought us. All glory is His. Put another way: Get over yourself, already!

2. **Boldness in Christ** – He has bought and equipped us for His purpose and mission. He has done these things perfectly; we are without excuse.

3. **Fidelity to the Gospel** – We have a duty to honor our King by proclaiming and defending His brutal, hated-by-the-world Gospel in its full, undiluted form.

INTRODUCTION

We must remember that we were once just as dead in rebellion as any false convert, false prophet, or apostate teacher has ever been. And while this should make us gracious, kind, and even loving to His enemies (and ours), it in no way gives us license to adopt worldly definitions of grace, kindness or love as a way of avoiding or deflecting His definitions of those terms and applying them to the defense of His truth as He has commanded. We have been supernaturally saved for His purpose, and He has made plain that this purpose includes our proclamation and defense of His truth.

We are to do this with boldness and clarity, and we will suffer for our obedience to Him in this calling. We will be hated for it. We will lose family and friend relationships over it. And He will be glorified through all of this...which is the whole point.

Only with these truths embraced can we fully understand and obey His call to an action fueled by righteous anger regarding the false religion of American Churchianity.

In *Apathetic Christianity*, we will explore several biblical reasons for this righteous anger of God's people against the zombie religion of American Churchianity, including:

Its adoption of secular principles and plans aimed squarely at deposing the family as the God-ordained center stage for worship and primary staging ground for worldwide evangelism, replacing it with...you guessed it..."church".

Its deep desire to be loved by the world. You know, the world that hates God, holiness, truth, and those who love and stand for the same. That world.

Its obsessive drive to make the dead in sin comfortable on their way to Hell (and doubly so if they "tithe" reliably on their way down).

HELL'S ESCORT SERVICE

"Not everyone who says to me, 'Lord, Lord,' will enter the kingdom of heaven, but the one who does the will of my Father who is in heaven. On that day many will say to me, 'Lord, Lord, did we not prophesy in your name, and cast out demons in your name, and do many mighty works in your name?' And then will I declare to them, 'I never knew you; depart from me, you workers of lawlessness.'"

Jesus (The Real One) in Matthew 7:21-23

And by this we know that we have come to know him, if we keep his commandments. Whoever says "I know him" but does not keep his commandments is a liar, and the truth is not in him"

1 John 2:3-4

Few systems of religion throughout recorded human history have been more effectively crafted to churn out the "workers of lawlessness" described by Jesus in the seventh chapter of Matthew than that of contemporary American Churchianity. It really does seem to have the whole black art of false assurance mastered; its capacity to comfortably escort millions to hell is without limit (or conscience).

When we use terms like "millions of workers of lawlessness", it's easy to lose sight of the fact that these doomed groups are composed of precious, loved individuals who are each made

INTRODUCTION

in the image of our holy God. Some are religious and some are secular. Some are our family members and some are strangers. Some are our friends and some are our enemies (whom we are to love). They are men, women, boys, and girls who, without the supernatural cure with which we have been entrusted and which we have been called to bring to them, are destined to face the eternal condemnation that we all once deserved.

They are teachers and preachers and pilots and homemakers. They are athletes and artists and leaders and soldiers. They are in your circle of friends and they are in your local congregation. They even sometimes share a cup of coffee with you while telling you how doomed they are and how comfortable they feel about it. They won't quite put it that way, of course, but, more often than not, you need neither pry hard nor peer intensely into their soul in order to see the truth that they tend to parade about quite effortlessly:

They are lost.

They are going to Hell.

And they are quite content.

Their religious leaders are paving this path to darkness and nurturing that contentedness, patting them supportively on the back as they take each successive step toward eternal damnation. Without divine intervention, these escorts to Hell will succeed. Fortunately, our Lord has just that sort of intervention in mind...through His chosen and obedient people.

His people and their love first for Him and then for the lost that He has called them to reach with His truth will be all that is needed here. This supernatural love and the action it inspires really is enough.

But wait, it gets better...and more challenging.

Not only does this supernatural weapon of liberation from slavery to sin and death known as the Gospel of Jesus Christ have the power to free the slaves of American Churchianity, it even has the power to save those who are at the helm – holding the wheel and guiding the ship, so to speak – of this God-forsaken system of man-obsessed religion. Yes, even the very escorts to Hell themselves can be freed from bondage and brought from death unto life, if only we will honor our King and proclaim His Gospel command to Hell's escorts along with their (temporary) captives.

The challenge here again is to remember that the worst of this zombie religion's gatekeepers is no closer to spiritual life than you or I were before He brought us from death to that life.

Really.

And we must act accordingly.

So when a guy like Rob Bell says something stupid and dangerous – and he will – remember: There but by the grace of God go *I*.

Same goes for Joel Osteen, Rick Warren, and the rest of the "top-tier" – or any tier, for that matter – cast of characters in the American Churchianity line-up.

They are our targets, along with their followers.

They are all targets for conversion.

INTRODUCTION

APATHY IS FOR LOSERS

This charge I entrust to you, Timothy, my child, in accordance with the prophecies previously made about you, that by them you may wage the good warfare, holding faith and a good conscience. By rejecting this, some have made shipwreck of their faith, among whom are Hymenaeus and Alexander, whom I have handed over to Satan that they may learn not to blaspheme.

1 Timothy 1:18-20

Vince Lombardi, the legendary head coach of the Green Bay Packers, once said, "Show me a good loser, and I'll show you a loser." In this, he seems to prophetically identify the heart of a problem that has left actual Christians either foundering or floating aimlessly in a sea that has come to be dominated and defined by American Churchianity.

We will not confront error.

We will not take stands.

We will not name names.

We will not obey our King's command to fight the good fight, wage the good warfare, and tear down enemy strongholds, bringing all things into submission under Christ.

And why won't we do these things?

'Cause they're "not nice".

They're hard.

And we have become, as Lombardi described, losers.

We're good at losing.

We like it. A lot. You might even say that, in many instances, we've come to love losing.

We definitely love it when we think it makes us look more humble or gracious or kind in the eyes of the world. And we really love to lose when fighting to win as He has commanded would actually cost us something we treasure – something we idolize – like status or peace or friendship or opportunity.

In this we have become that which we are called to destroy. We've become apathetic. In becoming apathetic we've become "good losers" from the world's perspective, which makes us just plain losers from a Christ-centered perspective.

So now it is time to get with the program.

His program – a program for warfare.

Total warfare.

Warfare with a purpose.

His purpose. And His ultimate victory.

WAGING THE GOOD (AND SUPERNATURAL) WARFARE

> *For though we walk in the flesh, we are not waging war according to the flesh. For the weapons of our warfare are not of the flesh but have divine power to destroy strongholds. We destroy arguments and every lofty opinion raised against the knowledge of God, and take every thought captive to obey Christ*
>
> 2 Corinthians 10:3-5

INTRODUCTION

We will not settle.

We will not compromise.

And we will not imagine for a moment that there is or was ever anything inherent within us that made us more worthy of salvation than any other zombie that there ever was.

We are here to win His promised victory by His grace and for His glory, and we will prevail against the very gates of Hell in the process. We will tear down every enemy stronghold between this place and that, grinding its ruins under our heels as we go on marching and bringing the walking dead to life in our wake. Our war against the zombie religion of Apathetic Christianity will be unlimited in its Christ-defined scope and unrelenting in securing its Christ-centered goals, because this is the only warfare that we can truly know as supernatural soldiers of the Sovereign King.

As we contemplate in these volumes the many battles that have come and gone, the battles that are upon us now, and the battles yet to come, we will examine several critical attributes and consequences of the religion of the enemy, including:

- **Apathetic Leadership** – Pastors, preachers, teachers, and leaders who scratch the "itching ears" of those who seek comfort apart from the Gospel of Christ and, in doing so, serve as willful escorts to Hell.

- **Apathetic Family Life** – Zombie religion's abandonment of (and hostility toward) the family as the centerpiece for worship and development of true sons and daughters of Christ.

- **Apathetic Education** – Zombie religion's embrace of

nearly every secular standard and principle of anti-Christian indoctrination in the name of "education".

- **Apathetic Theology and Doctrine** – Zombie religion's growing disdain for sound doctrine and theology…and her growing adoration of all things "relevant" and hip.

- **Apathetic Discipline** – Zombie religion's abandonment of biblical discipline and the unrestrained, immature-at-best hordes that naturally result.

- **Apathetic Politics** – Zombie religion's embrace of such "progressive" notions as the obliteration of the God-ordained/defined institution of marriage and the "right" to intentionally target an innocent child for murder.

Ultimately, as we are about the business of securing the promised victory of our King, we will culminate this work by examining, exalting and celebrating the unstoppable, supernatural weapon with which we have been equipped to secure the sure and never-ending conquest to come: The perfect, whole, undiluted Gospel of Jesus Christ.

So pray hard, stay frosty, and saddle up.

Today we ride…

…it's time to go zombie hunting…by His grace and for His glory…

SECTION 1

THE ZOMBIE RELIGION OF AMERICAN CHURCHIANITY

1

PASTOR FEELGOOD
AND HIS ALL-AMERICAN SALVATION MACHINE

HE WILL FEEL YOUR NEEDS AND FEED YOUR FLESH

> *For the time is coming when **people will not endure sound teaching**, but having itching ears **they will accumulate for themselves teachers to suit their own passions**, and will turn away from listening to the truth and wander off into myths.*
>
> 2 Timothy 4:3-4 (bold emphasis added)

"If Jesus had preached the same message that ministers preach today, He would never have been crucified."

Leonard Ravenhill

"My *God*…" the man let slip as he took in the image before him.
He and a fellow military intelligence operative sat at the table, looking down at a sketch in the old book as they sat there in the university library. Two professors stood looking on from across the

room, where the four had come seeking seclusion for a conversation of significant importance.

And secrecy.

"Yes, that's just what the Hebrews thought." Dr. Brody answered matter-of-factly as he walked slowly toward the table where the increasingly intrigued agents were sitting.

"What's that supposed to be coming out of there?" the second intelligence officer asked.

"Lightning. Fire. The power of God or something." Dr. Jones responded from behind Brody, standing just in front of a large rolling blackboard.

The first officer spoke again, this time in a more deliberate, concerned tone: "I'm beginning to understand Hitler's interest in this."

"Oh yes. The Bible speaks of the ark leveling mountains, laying waste to entire regions." Brody explained, "An army which carries the ark before it is invincible."

So begins Indiana Jones' fabled quest in *Raiders of the Lost Ark*, the runaway hit and pop-culture staple that first graced the silver screen in 1981. Steven Spielberg's and George Lucas' star-powered cinematic collaboration struck many chords with many people on its way to its current iconic status.

For all of the considerable success resulting from those well played chords, one truth that the film simultaneously confirmed and relied upon, perhaps unintentionally, was its exposition of the nature of man's regard for God – when he regards God at all, that is.

The idea is basically this: God is a tool.

Man's tool, to be precise.

This was the *Raiders'* plot lynch-pin delivered via Indiana Jones' friend Dr. Marcus Brody:

Hitler could manipulate the supernatural power of God if only he could find and control the ark. God's power would then become the ultimate point-and-shoot weapon in the hands of a presumably invincible Nazi army. Thus it is clear that any man – Nazi or otherwise – can tap into the unstoppable, unmatchable, supernatural power of God and manipulate it to his ends…if only he has the right tool or mechanism by which to do so.

In effect, through this realization you become god-like, or, for all practical purposes, God Himself. You realize that the tool is attainable by you, you seize the tool, and you use it as you please. In this, you ascend to the throne, take your seat, and direct His power – now your own – by your will, according to your desires, and for your ends.

Pretty neat, huh?

But hey, this is just the movies, right? I mean, should we be bothering reading so much into a Hollywood production when it comes to the nature of man, God, supernatural power, and the like? *Raiders of the Lost Ark* was a good flick and all, but does its little pitch and perspective on these subjects *really* matter?

Yes.

Really.

You see, sadly enough, the "Any man can claim, own, and control the power of God through tools" philosophy so central to *Raiders* is essentially the same view of God that is embraced and exalted by most of those leading the zombie religion movement in America.

In a very real sense *Raiders* is, at its heart, just another zombie flick.

Just as the Nazis fell under the spell of the charismatic Adolf Hitler, so too do the undead hordes of American Churchianity have their need-feeling, flesh-loving leaders. And, like Hitler, these leaders have an almost magical ability to captivate an audience and build a movement – a ministry, if you will – by appealing to the "itching ears" of the living dead.

And what do those ears most want to hear?

THE ZOMBIE RELIGION OF AMERICAN CHURCHIANITY

What do zombies assume to be true, yet yearn to have confirmed? Why, that they are actually *alive*, of course. Zombies want to be saved, or so they will often say. And many think that they are. Yet they are, and they most certainly wish to remain, zombies.

They love the flesh.

They live for it.

They feed it and feed on it; they can imagine nothing else. And it is in turn that the leaders of American Churchianity feed on them, by feeling their needs, feeding their flesh, and leading them straight to Hell and judgment, most often with a big smile, a kind word, and a warm, friendly pat on the back. If nothing else, the leaders of the Church of the Living Dead are masters of two things:

Deception and encouragement.

I'm Okay, You're Okay, and Nobody Goes to Hell

"For from the least to the greatest of them,
   everyone is greedy for unjust gain;
and from prophet to priest,
   everyone deals falsely.
They have healed the wound of my people lightly,
   saying, 'Peace, peace,'
   when there is no peace.
Were they ashamed when they committed abomination?
   No, they were not at all ashamed;
   they did not know how to blush.
Therefore they shall fall among those who fall;
   at the time that I punish them, they shall be overthrown," says the LORD.

Jeremiah 6:13-15

"A popular evangelist reaches your emotions. A true prophet reaches your conscience."

Leonard Ravenhill

"God isn't mad at anyone."

Tyler Padgitt

Can you pick out which of the above three quotes is "not like the others", as the Sesame Street song used to ask? Any wild guesses as to which one of the above speakers is the odd man out?

THE ZOMBIE RELIGION OF AMERICAN CHURCHIANITY

If you pegged "Tyler Padgitt", you win the prize, and the prize is the answer to the likely accompanying question: "Who is Tyler Padgitt?"

For every big-timey Joel Osteen type out there doing their best to spin Christianity into something much more appealing/comforting to unrepentant men and women on a global level, there are a gajillion less-known/talented Scripture-shredding wannabes out there doing the same sort of damage at a more local level. Tyler is one such small-scale zombie ministry builder.

He is the lead pastor of Truth Community Church in Springfield, Missouri, and he just loves to lift people up by bringing God down– ya know, knocking those unpleasant, inconvenient edges off so that He can be made more…appealing.

In Tyler World, God is not angry at anyone.

Really.

He only wants good things for you, don't ya know. He's like a nicer-than-Santa Santa that way.

Nothing very un-Osteen there…and that trend continues in almost every substantive sense. Tyler's real divergence from Joel comes in style, or lack thereof.

WHEN PIGS CAST "PEARLS"

"My sermon title will be *God is Not Mad at You*, and, uh, many people have that view of God – a view of God that I was taught about when I was a kid was that God was a fire-breathing menace who was looking for any excuse possible to punish you, and He would do so with much happiness and joy. And, uh, that's not the idea of God that I find from the Scriptures."

Pastor Tyler Padgitt, Truth Community Church,
Springfield, Missouri

"Beware of false prophets, who come to you in sheep's clothing but inwardly are ravenous wolves. You will recognize them by their fruits. Are grapes gathered from thornbushes, or figs from thistles? So, every healthy tree bears good fruit, but the diseased tree bears bad fruit. A healthy tree cannot bear bad fruit, nor can a diseased tree bear good fruit. **Every tree that does not bear good fruit is cut down and thrown into the fire.**"

Jesus (The Real One) in Matthew 7:15-19 (bold emphasis added)

See to it that no one takes you captive by philosophy and empty deceit, according to human tradition, according to the elemental spirits of the world, and not according to Christ.

Colossians 2:8

Another interesting feature of Tyler World's spin on zombie religion is that you are likely to hear pitched from his pulpit certain "intriguing" little tidbits that just don't seem to make it out of the mouths of more ready-for-prime-time zombie leaders.

For example, have you ever wondered what an Easter Sunday "sermon" including a more vivid description of violent diarrhea than the purpose of the crucifixion of Christ might sound like?

Nah, me neither...

Yet that's *exactly* what the good zombies at Truth Community Church in Springfield, Missouri, were treated to on Resurrection Day of 2011 (that is, when they weren't distracted by the big "Easter Egg" hunt).

And that wasn't all.

"Pastor" Tyler regaled the assembled horde with a hip(?) retelling of the story of David conveyed in 1 Samuel, which included the following gems:

- "And so one day this prophet-priest Samuel came to their house and said, "The Lord has called me to anoint a king for Israel out of your house." And so Jesse starts bringing out all his sons, and his sons are just incredible studs.

    I mean, they've got like, they're manicured, you know, they've got a lot of manscaping [?] done on their face. Some of them have blonde tips that have been dyed wonderfully and they come in with all of the spray tan on. They're like, "Hey, what's up?" and he's like, "No, not you."

The next guy comes along – he's hot [hawt?], he's handsome, he's good lookin', he's smart, he can play three different instruments at the same time. He's trying out for the priest, and he's like, "No, not you."

And so they go down this line of all these sons and none of them are chosen.

And so Samuel goes to Jesse and is like, "Hey, is there anybody else?" And he's like, "Pfffft! Yeah, there's David, but pfffft, this kid, you don't want him. He's out in the back forty tending my sheep, and he's singing with his harp love songs to this God of his, blowing kisses at Him. You don't want him; he's a weirdo."

He's like, "No. Bring him in."

And so here's David, the illegitimate child, unwanted, on the back forty, and he comes in, and the next thing ya know, the oil of the anointing is being poured on him, and he is destined by God to be the next king of Israel…That was 'Nacho Libre' in case you didn't know, the greatest film ever made.

"I'm concerned about you. You've not been baptized. You need to be baptized." If you don't know 'Nacho Libre' that wouldn't work for you, but if you do, that's very powerful. Yes, I know."

- "So David would come in with his harp, you know, the one that he sang out in the back forty with and he'd be there, and he'd be like, [begins to lay down a Lynyrd Skynyrd beat] "Sweet Home Jeeer-us-alem! Where the skies are so blue! Sweet Home Saul's Jerusalem! [crowd cheers] ..I'm coming home to you!"

And Saul'd be like, "Yeah!"

So that would work great for Saul and he began to depend on David. But then one day Saul just all of a sudden goes, "AaahhhhhhHHHHH, FREAK OUT!" [crowd laughs] and he takes this javelin, while David's in the corner singing "Sweet Home Jerusalem", and just [inserts sound effect] hurls it at poor little David."

- "David came to Nob to Ahimelech the priest. And Ahimelech came to meet David trembling and said to him, "Why are you alone? Why is there nobody with you?"

This is strange.

David's the anointed-to-be-king guy. Can you imagine Obama showing up, ya know, if you worked at a gas station and was like, "Can I have a Slurpee?"
Like, "Dude, where's the Secret Service? Where are your people?" Ya know?
Where's the dude with the football and the nuclear codes?"[1]

Lest there be any lingering doubt as to the context or truth of these excerpts as accurate representations of Tyler's magnificent *God is*

---

[1] Tyler Padgitt sermon: *God is not Mad at You*, taken from Truth Community Church web site (http://www.truthchurch.net/audio).

Not Mad at You show, the entire "sermon" is available for inspection at the Truth Community Church web site (with a direct link to the sermon posted at FireBreathingChristians.com).

You are strongly encouraged to read/listen through the entire thing.

While sitting down.

With some Tums nearby.

While wading through "sermon high points" from *God is Not Mad at You* can certainly be painful, this has been pain with a purpose. The purpose comes when we consider the following questions:

- Does "pastor" Tyler *revere* Scripture?
- Does "pastor" Tyler interpret modern culture in light of Scripture, or does he interpret Scripture in light of modern culture?
- Does "pastor" Tyler even know what Easter is, in a Christian context?

These are serious questions.

And just in case there was any confusion with where "pastor" Tyler comes down on the whole "righteous anger of a holy God against rebellious, unrepentant sinners" deal that is about as central as it gets to orthodox, biblical Christianity, he managed to chant his way into the close of the "sermon" with the following counter-Christian thought:

> "God's not mad at you.
> You just need to trust Him.
> God's not mad at you.
> You just need to trust him.
> God's not mad at you.
> You just need to trust Him..."

THE ZOMBIE RELIGION OF AMERICAN CHURCHIANITY

With all of this considered, how must we assume that those sitting under the teaching of "pastor" Padgitt and the thousands like him are likely to come to view matters of great consequence such as:

- The holiness of God.
- The sinfulness of man.
- The sacred nature of Scripture – and the reverence it must command.
- The righteous judgment to come against those who do not repent as the Gospel commands.

It is at least arguable that, though the likes of Joel Osteen, Rob Bell, Rick Warren & Company get much more press and are the modern faces of the zombie religion of American Churchianity, it is the Tyler Padgitts of the world – by their sheer numbers and sheer disregard for hard biblical attributes and truth – that do far more damage.

We must pray for them.

And confront them in the Spirit commanded and provided by our Lord.

As mentioned earlier, when it comes to method, style, and certainly message, Tyler is just one of thousands of lower level, localized leaders of zombie religion in America. As such, he's only mimicking what he sees at the top of the zombie food chain.

Speaking of zombiedom's favorite performers, one of the rock stars headlining at the Church of the Emergent Dead is a guy by the name of Rob Bell. Rob likes to deconstruct Christianity. A lot.

He's been on a nearly straight-down trajectory for many years now, heading, with his latest (and incredibly popular in American Churchianity) book release, *Love Wins*, straight into the domain of universalism, making the case against the orthodox Christian view on Hell.

Interestingly and ironically enough, he makes the case against Hell while simultaneously leading people there, so Rob is also into multitasking.

Yay Rob.

Like his books, Bell is wildly popular on the evangelical scene, and it's easy to see why. Among other things, he has that same warmed-over Santa of a God that most Pastor Feelgoods tend to build their imagined reality around.

Of course, en route to this land of fictional Santa Jesuses and unholy "love", Bell has to basically eviscerate scores of central core truths as revealed in Scripture.

But no biggie.

That sort of evisceration is an inherent specialty of each and every Pastor Feelgood.

Christian Pastor and teacher John MacArthur recently described Bell's brand of Bible-mutilating zombieism this way:

> Just how serious is Rob Bell's heresy? It is not merely that he rejects what Jesus taught about hell; *Bell rejects the God of Scripture.* He deplores the idea of divine vengeance against sin (Romans 12:9). He cannot stand the plain meaning of texts like Hebrews 12:29: "Our God is a consuming fire." He has no place in his thinking for the biblical description of Christ's fiery return with armies of angels: "dealing out retribution to those who do not know God and to those who do not obey the gospel of our Lord Jesus" (2 Thessalonians 1:7-8). Bell's whole message is a flat contradiction of Jesus' words in Luke 12:5: "But I will warn you whom to fear: fear the One who, after He has killed, has authority to cast into hell; yes, I tell you, fear Him!"
> Bell will have none of that. He therefore tries to eliminate the authority and clarity of Scripture so that he can

reinvent a god who is more to his liking. It is the sin of all sins; the sin of the serpent. Like Eve's tempter, Bell is subtly but undeniably fomenting rebellion against the true God. He suggests that he is *better*—nicer, more kindly, more tolerant, more lenient—than the God who has revealed Himself in Scripture. He therefore sets aside God's revealed Word and makes his own musings the inviolable standard.

In effect he wants to assume the role of God for himself. That is not a minor evil; it is epic. It is the original sin of Lucifer.

MacArthur puts his finger on the core component of Bell's – and all zombie religionist's – rotten worldview, namely that man is, at least practically speaking, his own god.

While Rob Bell is certainly a large and still-rising star in zombie religion, he's still got a bit to go to reach the top, also known as: Osteen Country.

"I Don't Know" the Gospel

> "As God can send a people or a nation no greater blessing than to give them faithful, upright and sincere ministers, so the greatest curse that God can possibly send upon the people of this world is to give them over to blind, unregenerate, carnal, lukewarm and unskilled guides."
>
> George Whitfield

In an appearance on CNN's Larry King Live[2], zombie herder extraordinaire Joel Osteen offered the following insight into his understanding of the nature of God, man, salvation and the Gospel:

Larry King: We've had ministers on who've said, *'Your record don't count. You either believe in Christ or you don't. If you believe in Christ, you are going to Heaven, and if you don't, no matter what you've done in your life, you ain't.'*

Smiling Osteen: Yeah, I don't know, it's – there's probably a balance between – I believe that you have to know Christ, but I think that if you know Christ, if you're a believer in God, then you're gonna have some good works. I think it's a copout to say, 'well, I'm a Christian, but I don't ever do anything to help people.

Larry King: What if you're a Jew or Muslim and you don't accept Christ at all?

---

[2] *Larry King Live* interview, viewable here: http://youtu.be/KwL1DThtxYg

Smiling Osteen: You know – I'm just, I'm very careful about saying who would and wouldn't go to Heaven. I think only God – [Larry interjects]

Larry King: You believe that you have to believe in Christ, so they're wrong aren't they?

Grinning Osteen: Well, I don't know if I believe they're wrong. I believe here's what the Bible teaches and from the Christian faith this is what I believe, but I just think that only God can judge a person's heart.

I've spent a lot of time in India with my father and, ya know, I don't know all about their religion, but I know they love God. And I don't know, I'd, uh, haveta – I've seen their sincerity, so I don't know, just, I know, for me, and what the Bible teaches, I want to have a relationship with Jesus.

Larry King (moving on to calls): Phoenix, Arizona, hello.

Caller: Hello Larry, you're the best and thank you Joel for your positive messages and your book. I'm wondering, though, why you side stepped Larry's earlier question about how we get to Heaven? The Bible clearly tells us that Jesus is the way, the truth, and the life, and the only way to the Father is through Him. That's not really a message of condemnation, but of truth.

Not-so-smiling Osteen: Yeah, I would agree with her. I believe...[Larry interjects]

Larry King: So then a Jew is not going to Heaven.

Really-not-smiling Osteen: No, I, I, well here's my thing, Larry: I can't judge someone's heart, you know? I don't know. Only God can look at somebody's heart, and so, I don't know, it's just, to me it's not my business to say that this one is or this one isn't. I'm just saying that here's what the Bible teaches, and I'm gonna put my faith in, you know, in Christ, and I think it's wrong to go around saying, 'You're not, you're not going, 'cause it's not exactly my way.'

Larry King: But you believe your way.

Flatlining Osteen: I believe my way with all my heart.

Larry King: So someone who doesn't share it…is wrong, aren't they?

Finished Osteen: Well, I don't know if I look at it like that. I would present my way, but I'm just gonna let God be the judge of that. **I don't know.**

And that, in a nutshell, is it: Joel…*doesn't*…*know*.
And he ain't foolin'.
He *really* doesn't know.
He doesn't know the God of the Bible enough to present Him to anyone.
He doesn't know the Gospel of Christ enough to present it to anyone.
And, worst of all, He doesn't know that he doesn't know *those things*, so along he goes, "preaching" a form of self-appeasing darkness all too familiar and comfortable to those who are already dead and will remain so outside of the power of the Gospel – you know, the Gospel that Joel & Friends never have to offer.

Yet while they don't have anything better than death to preach to the dead, Joel, Tyler, Rick, Rob and pals do indeed have some neat little extras with which to distract.

Things like self-esteem and self-empowerment.

Yes, they have those sorts of zombie-pleasing toys to offer by the truckload…

GOD AS YOUR BEST TOOL NOW

"All it takes is 1) seeing or visualizing whatever you need, whether physical or financial; 2) staking your claim on Scripture; and 3) speaking it into existence."

Kenneth Copeland

"The first step to living at your full potential is to *enlarge your vision*. To live your best life now, you must start looking at life through eyes of faith, seeing yourself rising to new levels. See your business taking off. See your marriage restored. See your family prospering. See your dreams coming to pass. You must conceive it and believe it is possible if you ever hope to experience it"

Joel Osteen

While one man's route to the manipulation of God's supernatural power might be the procurement of the ark of the covenant, another man's path of choice might be, say, positive thinking or positive speech or positive self-image or, well, pretty much anything positively man-centered.

God will do your bidding if you just know how to point him in the right direction…or pray using a particular formula…or visualize the right things in the right way…or say the right words with the right amount of right kind of sincerity…

The bottom line is: He is yours to command. You just need to learn the secret handshake.

This "God's power can be yours to command" notion was basically the view of Hitler according to the intelligence officers in *Raiders of the Lost Ark* and it is basically the view of such legendary contemporary zombie leaders as Joel Osteen, Benny Hinn, Kenneth Copeland, and Joyce Meyer.

This particular branch of zombie religion is generally known as the Word Faith movement, and while we will not cover the Word Faith system in detail here, the reader is encouraged to consult Hank Hanegraaff's *Christianity in Crisis*, as well as this author's own *Fire Breathing Christians* for a more detailed treatment of the subject.

At the end of the day, however, the grand strategies zombie religion's leadership all center on that one, critical, inescapable core component: An appeal to man as the determiner of his own fate, which is another way of saying, man as his own god.

This is the ultimate "felt need" of the zombie.

He just wants to "be his own man" and despises the thought of being anyone else's.

And what could be more All-American than that?

This ultimate felt need is the ultimate target of flesh-feeding Pastor Feelgoods spanning the spectrum from Tyler Padgitt to Joel Osteen.

From the springboard of the exaltation of man over God, all things become possible, many of which will be explored in the coming chapters, including:

- The mythical "Flu Shot Jesus" who saves forever without changing a thing.
- The equally nonsensical "Carnal Christian", who is the natural offspring of a Flu Shot Jesus encounter.
- The McGospel Plan of Salvation – "Just say this prayer, vote Flu Shot Jesus your savior and it'll all be good."
- The zombie-driven church – Where needs are felt and flesh is fed…all in Jesus' name.

In establishing and reinforcing these anti-Christian principles, characters, and concepts, Pastor Feelgoods throughout American Churchianity have convinced the walking dead that they are alive and safe when they are, in fact, dead in sin and standing on the verge of the righteous judgment of a holy God. They've demonstrated time and again a near total lack of reverence for Scripture, an open contempt for revealed truth, and a profound lack of respect for the Author of both.

And they've done it all with a smile.

2

THE PROBLEM WITH
DEAD PEOPLE

THE FUTILITY OF
ZOMBIE HERDING

2

THE PROBLEM WITH DEAD PEOPLE

THE FUTILITY OF ZOMBIE HERDING

"Wherever the natural will of man is spoken of in the Bible it is always spoken of as being a depraved will; a degenerate will; an evil, sinful will."

Jim McClarty

"Someone asked me, 'Do you pray for the dead?' I said, 'No, I preach to them!' I think every pew in every church is death row. Think about that! They're dead! They sing about God; they talk about God, but they're dead!"

Leonard Ravenhill

I can remember walking down to the front of the sanctuary at First Baptist Church of Ozark at the end of the worship service back in the spring of 2008. I was there to join the church and express publically to my new home crowd that I had a clear call into ministry. It was a very good moment.

Shortly after that formal connection with the local body, including the presentation of my calling to a particular sort of supercool spiritual path, I began meeting with pastors, teachers, and various other leaders within the FBCO organization. Everyone was nice. We talked. We prayed. Over the course of the next six months or so, I learned a lot about how certain things worked and what certain people thought within that local gathering of believers.

In the midst of this period of dramatic twists and turns in life, I finished writing *Fire Breathing Christians* and secured a contract to release the book through a well-known and highly regarded publisher. Things really seemed to be clicking.

I was thrilled and thankful to God to have had both the call toward this incredible new (and unexpected) direction in life and the external confirmation of not only a completed book, but a contract for its publication and release. Much was changing, and quickly. I was hoping and praying and, frankly, *expecting* that this would all tie in beautifully with First Baptist Church of Ozark.

But a funny thing happened on the way to "tie in with beautifully".

That thing was, ironically, *Fire Breathing Christians*. Or, more precisely, the ideas that motivated and permeated *Fire Breathing Christians*.

Apparently, "Reformation types" aren't viewed as prime – or secondary or tertiary – options for preaching, teaching, or pretty much any other position of service within the church through which other church members had a high likelihood of exposure to "those ideas".

And by those ideas, I mean:

- Man is evil. He hates God. He is born that way.

- Man is dead in sin and cannot see, much less *do* anything to positively interact with God or His Kingdom apart from the supernatural intervention of the very God he hates.

- The supernatural nature of the Gospel and salvation. Put another way, dead men don't "choose" God because dead men are dead men. God saves them so that then, as supernaturally created "new creatures" in Christ with a new nature, they then choose Him out of love and adoration just as naturally as they had previously chosen precisely the opposite route.

It was this whole "supernatural" angle that seemed to acutely aggravate one particular church staff member of influence, who said one time in response to the suggestion that true salvation was a supernatural act: "I have no idea what you're talking about."

And, believe me, he really didn't.

The notion of a "supernatural act of salvation" was about the weirdest, most foreign thing that had ever been brought to the attention of this…church *leader*.

Back-Stroking in the Punch Bowl

"I believe every church is either supernatural or superficial. I don't believe there's any middle ground."

Leonard Ravenhill

"If we retain only what can be justified by standards of prudence and convenience at the bar of enlightened common sense, then we exchange revelation for that old wraith Natural Religion."

C.S. Lewis

The more I read, the more I learned, the more I grew, and the more I wrote, the more trouble I seemed to be in on the FBCO front. Not that anyone was overtly mean to me. Quite the contrary; they were usually very sweet and kind. It's just that the more of what I wrote and thought got around, the less I seemed to fit within the acceptable parameters set by what I was only then coming to recognize as the guiding of principles for that particular church, namely:

1. Numbers, numbers, numbers. The number is to purpose-driven churches like FBCO what location is to real estate.
2. Purpose-driven business models must be used to attain the desired numbers.
3. More purpose-driven business models must be used to sustain the desired numbers.

So, when I wrote a book proclaiming:

1. The horror of a numbers, numbers, numbers obsession that produces slavery to secular ideals in the place of slavery to Christ and Scripture.

2. The horror of a purpose-driven business model approach to all things "church".

3. The horror of selling Flu Shot Jesus as a part of the McGospel model of evangelism.

   …and…

4. In reaction to the above three "horrors", the need for a modern day reformation, revival, and revolution in the family, the church, and the culture…

…well, let's just say my "Mr. Popularity" ranking was taking a pretty vicious beat down on a near-weekly basis there at good ol' FBCO.

"Reformers" just didn't have the qualities that a church like FBCO was looking for. Pretty much any thought I articulated in detail seemed to clash with the core guiding philosophies of the church. So, the more I wrote and spoke and shared, the less appealing I became.

And the less appealing FBCO became to me.

All by God's grace and for His glory.

THE PROBLEM WITH DEAD PEOPLE

"God saved you for Himself; God saved you by Himself; God saved you from Himself."

Paul Washer

"God doesn't choose those who would choose Him. He chooses those who would never choose Him."

Mark Driscoll

So it is that, in a purpose-driven world, Reformation types have some serious baggage. They're just loaded with unattractive features.

Similarly, though I hope not-quite-identically, zombies are not exactly known for their positive or endearing qualities.

While the less-than-appealing side of the zombie attributes ledger is as long as the "Cool things about being a zombie" side is short, the big, bad, inescapably significant problem-of-all-problems facing those who have a zombie fetish is that those potential pew and coffer filling creatures have one, *ahem*, *fatal* flaw:

They're dead.

Really dead. Totally and completely dead-ola.

"D-E-D, dead", as the movie goes.

And dead means dead.

They're not kinda dead, or getting close to deadness or on the verge of deaditude or any such thing.

They. Are. Dead.

Okay, see if this helps:

Imagine a zombie.

Now imagine *Enterprise* chief medical guy Dr. McCoy looking at Captain Kirk while pointing to the zombie and speaking very clearly:

"He's dead, Jim!"

Is it clicking into place yet?

Did the visualization help?

Are you getting it?

I mean you, Rick…Joel…Rob…Benny…

…and every zombie herder following your lead.

Of course, the answer to all of the above on the deadness of the dead and its meaning (that the dead are dead) is a simple, clear, "Nope."

Or, more accurately, "*Heck nope!*"

Even with the McCoy/Kirk illustration. That's how irresistible these zombies are to some.

After all, these zombies laugh. They smile. They sign up for programs. They even *run* programs. And that's not all.

They write books for Christians, teach classes for Christians, manage ministries for Christians, run seminaries for Christians…there really is nothing that these zombies won't do if we just let 'em. In many cases, it's as though they're just waiting to jump right in – pounce, if you will – and make the church their own.

All they ask in return is that we feed their flesh.

And feeding the flesh, when you're a seeker-sensitive, media-savvy, culture-following, purpose-driven kinda church, is oh…so…*easy*.

Practical, too.

It just seems to come naturally, really.

Precisely because it is natural.

For zombies.

THE DEVIL'S FAVORITE ZOMBIE FLICK

"All you have to do is get in a closer walk with God and you'll find your enemies are in your own church."

Leonard Ravenhill

"False teachers are God's judgment upon people who don't want God, but in the name of religion plan on getting everything their carnal heart desires. That's why a Joel Osteen is raised up. Those people who sit under him are not victims of his; he is the judgment of God upon them."

Paul Washer

As the saying goes, if you're gonna do something, you should always strive to be the very best at it. Be the best at whatever you do!

You can't get more American than that, can you?

With this standard as a guide, I think it more than fair and accurate to say that contemporary American Churchianity has shot to and right on through the top of the charts where both quantitative and qualitative measurements of zombie herding "success" are concerned.

Just think about it:

Quantitatively, we have millions upon millions of zombies - more zombies than ever assembled in Jesus' name before – roaming the halls and centers of thousands upon thousands of church-like buildings all across the fruited plain. They join programs, support ministries, start ministries, run ministries, and fill the vast majority of pews within the vast majority of church-like organizations in the nation.

And *qualitatively*, we have all sorts of good zombie folk *leading* religious movements and ministries. They teach, preach, write, and guide. They are, in many if not most cases, the leaders of the "church".

It is this combination of quantitative and qualitative "excellence in zombie attraction" that has made American Churchianity what she is today.

In the spirit of giving credit where credit is due, let's be clear: **American Churchianity has done more than any other force in the culture to make America what she is today.**

Consider the flesh feeding fruits of this modern American religion:

- It has intentionally displaced the family as God's primary ordained institutional center-place for His worship.
- It has intentionally embraced practically every counter-Christian, Madison Avenue spun approach to marketing that has come down the pike.
- It has intentionally dismissed the supernatural Gospel of Christ in an effort to appeal to those who hate Him.
- And, as has been established but is certainly worth repeating here: It has intentionally done all of these things *in Jesus' name*.

Considering the sheer scale of this obviously quite purpose-driven operation, has there ever been an institution operating at anywhere near this level of success where the implementation of systemized blasphemy is concerned?

Zombie herding…escorting tens of millions to Hell…in Jesus' name.

Let that soak in.

THE ZOMBIE RELIGION OF AMERICAN CHURCHIANITY

Modern America has voluntarily made itself the real-time stage and setting for Satan's favorite zombie flick. And modern American religion is this film's producer.

At the end of the day, the zombie herding Pastor Feelgood types leading American Churchianity have left the Devil with precious little to worry about aside from what to snack on while he watches. Get him some popcorn and a Coke and he's pretty much set.

(Please sit down, Rob...that was a joke...sort of...)

3

FLU SHOT JESUS
CANDY CHRISTIANITY'S MAGICAL SUPERPAL

AMERICA'S FAVORITE ANTI-CHRIST

FLU SHOT JESUS
CANDY CHRISTIANITY'S MAGICAL SUPERPAL

AMERICA'S FAVORITE ANTI-CHRIST

*Do not marvel at this, for an hour is coming when all who are in the tombs will hear his voice and come out, those who have done good to the resurrection of life, and **those who have done evil to the resurrection of judgment**.*

John 5:28-29 (bold emphasis added)

"God's not mad at you."

Tyler Padgitt (nothing bold to emphasize)

"...American Christianity has designed itself as self-help therapy with a little Jesus thrown in. [It] has become nothing more than another vehicle for you to feel good about yourself, and I'm telling you: You will 'feel good about yourself' all the way to Hell.

This is not funny. **God is the judge of all the earth and He will do right. And if you continue on this quest for [your personal] significance, He will do what is right. He will view you as a rebel...He will consider you an enemy and He will judge you.**"

S. Michael Durham (bold truth emphasized)

On March 11, 2011, in what has come to be known as "The Great East Japan Disaster", a 9.0 magnitude earthquake – the most powerful ever known to have hit Japan – struck off the coast of Oshika Peninsula. It produced a catastrophic tsunami. Within minutes of the tragic event's opening act, the modern age of instant access and free flowing information made its presence as plain as the quake itself. Videos streamed from cell phones and Twitter feeds relayed details in near real-time. The Japanese Apocalypse seemed to have its own Fox News theme music before the buildings had even stopped shaking.

Adding to the horror of an already catastrophic event, the Fukushima Nuclear Power Plant was compromised and ultimately failed, prompting Japan to declare a state of emergency. European Energy Commissioner Gunther Oettinger, in an address to the European Parliament on March 15, described the event as an "apocalypse".

In the wake of all of this, Western media seemed to be conflicted as to how serious the nuclear portion of the earthquake disaster really was. Some predicted doom, proclaiming imminent meltdown at the failed Fukushima facilities, while others treated the whole nuclear part of Japan's trouble as no big deal at all.

Nothing to see here...and, heck, the radiation might even be good for you. (It worked wonders for Godzilla, after all.)

Environmental activist groups suffered little of the "conflicted" affliction that had beset the media, however. They rocketed into action, protesting the evils of nuclear power almost as quickly as Fox News had the Japanese Apocalypse theme music up and rolling.

In the midst of all of this, I was living in Seattle, wondering, among other things, who was right on the nuclear analysis. Was the cloud of leaked radioactivity that was heading across the Pacific really the black hand of death that some were painting it to be, or was it the practical equivalent of a mass of airborne vitamin C as some extremely pro-nuke types seemed to imply?

While I had never really been a vitamin supplement kind of guy, after reading up on the situation I decided that it might be a good idea to start down that path, what with the black cloud of nuclear powered death heading Seattle way and all. So off to several downtown health-food-ish stores I went, picking out what was my first official collection of daily vitamins not to be found in a cheeseburger, pizza, or some similarly bachelor-friendly bit of culinary wonder.

It was a few days later – well into establishing my new daily vitamin routine as a habit – that I noticed something peculiar while perusing the aisles at the local Safeway. Something *very* peculiar…

I was happily be-bopping along, pushing my cart along ahead of me, when I noticed something green. A whole lot of green, actually. There was lettuce, celery, cucumbers, apples. There was a jar of pickles. And around the green were splashes of strawberry red and banana yellow. Very festive, I thought, but also very…weird.

What made all of this more than a little odd was that these natural shades of green, red and yellow were all in *my* shopping cart. Apparently, I had just happened to go about the process of shopping in auto-pilot mode and, for the first time in my life, I had only fruits and vegetables in there. I was stunned.

I even stopped in the middle of the realization to snap a picture of the cart with my iPhone.

This was a big deal.

Before any Greenpeaceniks or McDonald's Haters out there who happen to be reading this get too awful excited, rest assured (or disappointed) in the fact that, before I left Safeway on that day, I had added Cheetos, Twinkies, and a handful of other "normal" items to my haul. Still, the whole thing represented quite a shift.

I finished that weekend on a true, first-time-for-me surge into healthhood. It felt good...at least in my mind...at least for that weekend.

Three days into this vitamin and vegetable fueled approach to life (combined with my already established routine of walking 10+ miles each day), I felt invincible, or at least on the verge of it.

Then, on Day Four, my magic carpet ride to healthiness crashed, and hard, with me coming down with the most annoying conflagration of respiratory and digestive disorders that I can remember facing at any one time. It was ridiculous.

Of course, I instantly blamed the vegetables. And if it wasn't the vegetables, it had to be some weird sort of chemical reaction that occurred when vegetables were combined with vitamins. Yeah, it had to be one of those two things.

Having been blessed with good health (if I take Tylenol more than twice a year, it's an "off year" for me), I was so certain that the switch from health-light to health-heavy intake would bump me up to the next level that I couldn't even imagine the opposite outcome as a likely outcome for anyone taking this route, much less the one that I would experience.

Yet there it was – my vitamin and veggie packed body was as bad off as it'd been in years – decades, even. The Greens had lied. The Health Nuts were just plain nuts. The more I type, the sillier I feel for having ever even entertained the notion that they were on to something – anything – good.

I should have known better.

And why fiddle with a smoothly operating machine like my largely taco- and Dunkin' Donuts-fueled self, anyway? My lifelong strategy of creating a personal biological environment so overtly hostile to potential invaders that no germ or virus with even the slightest sense of self-preservation would dare even *consider* trespassing on – or in – my turf, had clearly worked. And well. For years and years and years.

Then I bought the lie; the veggie and vitamin lie.

Apparently, I had to learn the hard way.

In all seriousness, while health food and vitamins are actually wonderful things, and maintaining our bodies is an important aspect of our fidelity to and glorification of God, there is no doubt that fallen men and women are very susceptible to deception; particularly deception that has already proven popular with others. Promises of an easy path to a wonderful destination are quite naturally a great temptation to us, and all the more so when we see friends and family stampeding in that direction.

CHEAP + EASY = RED FLAG

> "The greatest heresy in the American Evangelical and Protestant church is that if you pray and ask Jesus Christ to come into your heart, He will definitely come in."
>
> Paul Washer

> "The sinner's prayer has sent more people to Hell than all the taverns in America."
>
> Leonard Ravenhill

We love beautiful things, and that tends to be good.

We also love easy things, and that tends to be bad.

With this in mind, it's no surprise that the enemy would aim to craft a counterfeit of the most beautiful thing (Christ) by attaching a perverted version of it (or Him) to our inherent love of ease.

What could be more appealing than a Jesus who has only *your* happiness in mind? What could be more attractive than a Jesus who lives only to serve *your* desires right where they are? What could be more wonderful than a Jesus who conforms his will to yours and uses all of his power accordingly?

How about one who will give you *all* of these things – fulfill all of your desires – without expecting anything of you or even slightly nudging you to change anything at all? In other words: A Jesus who doesn't judge, or, as Tyler Padgitt likes to say, a Jesus who "isn't mad at anyone."

What self-centered rebel wouldn't want a "savior" who saves them from Hell *and* from any pressure to change or conform to any standard outside of their own?

Sound too good to be true, non-believer?

Not so!

This "savior" is very real...at least in the minds of men. He feels *good*. Very good. Sinfully so, some might say. And you can find him headlining every Sunday in the auditoriums of American Churchianity. He loves those big stages, and he knows how to play a crowd. He's been perfecting his game for thousands of years.

Enter: Flu Shot Jesus.

THE PROBLEM WITH IMAGINARY FRIENDS

"When people say, 'I believe in Jesus', look them straight in the eye and ask, 'Which one?'"

Walter Martin

...he asked his disciples, "Who do people say that I am?" And they told him, "John the Baptist; and others say, Elijah; and others, one of the prophets." And he asked them, "But who do you say that I am?"

Mark 8:27-29

In America, practically everybody knows Jesus. And most claim to like the guy or even love him. And how could they not? After all, this Jesus that the typical everyman in America seems to regard highly sure has all the right positions on all the right issues, including:

1. **Jesus knows that men and women are basically good.** Sure, they mess up sometimes, but nobody's perfect, Jesus understands this, and he just wants to help people do better by guiding them from mediocre to good, good to better, and better to best.
2. **Jesus is love** – with love meaning whatever you want it to mean, so long as it requires of Jesus that...:
    - ...he'll never personally punish/discipline you.
    - ...he'll never be angry with you personally.
    - ...he'll never "force himself" anywhere that you don't want him to be.

3. **Jesus just wants you to let him help you.** He respects your authority over your own life and would never even think of transgressing on your autonomy, but he would really like it if you'd choose to let him in the door, so to speak, so he can make your life better.

4. **Jesus, if you'll just let him "into your heart"** (whatever that means) **and say one time a few key words, will stamp both your Get Out of Hell Free and Free Pass to Heaven cards**...simultaneously! These stamps never expire. They seal you entirely and allow you to go about your business as before without worrying at all about where you're going when you die.

5. **Jesus will demand nothing of you after you vote him in as savior.** He's just happy to have you and has no serious expectations beyond that. That's just the kind of Jesus that he is.

If there's one thing that comes through with crystal clarity where the nature of this Jesus is concerned, it's that he is all about **you**.

He submits to your will. He is there to help (and never punish or criticize). His only real aim is to gently encourage you toward your best possible life, both here and hereafter.

How cool is that!

Whatta deal!

Now this is a Jesus that sells! This Jesus has real appeal in a culture like ours. He is imminently marketable; just seems to "sell himself", so to speak. He seems to have it all – everything attractive and good to offer with none of the drawbacks.

Kinda like Coke Zero.

But this Jesus does have one little problem – a single lingering issue that does tend to paint all of this theoretical wonder in a different light. You see, unlike Coke Zero, this Jesus doesn't actually exist.

He isn't real.

He's a fiction.

In this, he is just as credible as a savior as the equally fictitious Jesuses of Mormonism, Islam, or *The Big Lebowski*.

Flu Shot Jesus – the centerpiece prop of contemporary evangelical American Churchianity – is, at the end of the day, nothing more than *the most widely adored, cherished, and promoted imaginary friend in human history*.

He is fiction.

And fiction can't save anybody...even if it makes 'em feel really, really good.

MEET THE *OTHER* OTHER JESUS

> "We regard God as an airman regards his parachute; it's there for emergencies but he hopes he'll never have to use it."
>
> C.S. Lewis, *The Problem of Pain*

> *...But for the sake of the elect those days will be cut short. Then if anyone says to you, 'Look, here is the Christ!' or 'There he is!' do not believe it. For false christs and false prophets will arise...*
>
> Matthew 24:22-24

Prior to the advent of American Churchianity, it was uncommon for imaginary friends to run in packs. But as anyone who's made a study of Flu Shot Jesus quickly discovers, he has a friend. Yes, an imaginary friend with an imaginary friend...and you thought the zombie theme was weird...

Yet there he is, this *other* other Jesus, paving the way for his Flu Shot buddy when possible, and distracting unsuspecting zombies 'till it's too late when he's not.

He's the one you keep hearing about knocking on your door. Not that you hear the actual knock, mind you, but you always seem to hear about it. 'Specially during those altar calls.

He's the guy who's always there waiting for you; making himself available for activation any time you're ready.

He is there to save you on your command, and is perfectly content to sit silently and smile while waiting for that command.

He is, of course, Ripcord Jesus.

Activating Your Imaginary Savior

"None is righteous, no, not one;
  no one understands;
  no one seeks for God.
All have turned aside; together they have become worthless;
  no one does good,
  not even one."

Romans 3:10-12

"But the sons of this world have not God; they have only each other, and they walk holding to each other and looking to one another for assurance like frightened children."

A.W. Tozer

For those who somehow manage to resist the pull of that 342nd repetition of the last verse of *Just as I Am* during a typical contemporary American Churchianity altar call, they are almost always sent home from the show with the promise of Ripcord Jesus riding their shoulder home.

The Ripcord pitch goes something like this:

"For those of you struggling or wondering or waiting, please pray and know that Jesus is waiting on you. He is with you. He will obey your command to save when you're ready to give it."

Okay, that last sentence probably wouldn't be spoken quite that way, but the precise sentiment contained therein would indeed be conveyed. The idea is simple: Jesus saves at your command. He is powerless over your will and is therefore content to wait for you to come around. While waiting, he is there to smile, encourage and generally do the nice things you'd expect of a competent politician running for an office that holds more power than he has now.

He's your buddy.

He's your pal.

He really, really likes you!

And man, does he ever want - and would really appreciate – your vote.

There he sits…on your shoulder…waiting…waiting for you to die.

Oops! Was that last part out loud?

The "waiting for you to die" part, I mean.

Well, since it's slipped out there, we might as well explain…

You see, the *actual* mission of Ripcord Jesus is the provision of false security through the presentation of a false option.

By allowing a zombie to nurture the mirage of salvation-on-command, Ripcord Jesus allows said zombie to continue in his flesh-feeding lifestyle with abandon, operating as though he can safely continue on his natural destructive path of self-indulgence while always having the "magic salvation button" to push when/if he finds himself in a tough spot.

Here's a handy, generic checklist that can be helpful in identifying one's probable status as a fooled follower of Ripcord Jesus:

1. You are open to sexual purity *later*, but for now you want to "have your fun".
2. You are open to avoiding drunkenness later, but for now you want to "have your fun".
3. You are open to reading terribly boring books like the Bible later, but for now you want to "have your fun".
4. You are open to letting Jesus save you later, and like the fact that he's there waiting, but for now you want to "have your fun".

If any of the first three (or similar) points apply to you, *and* the fourth one fits as well, then you almost certainly are a fooled follower of Ripcord Jesus. And despite what you've been taught by the zombie religionists of the age, Ripcord Jesus is no more real than Flu Shot Jesus. They are lies. Useful lies for some, but lies nonetheless.

Yet both are actively, vigorously, and very successfully promoted from the pulpits and through the ministries of American Christianity.

In the next chapter, we will take a closer look at just how that is done...and why the whole dark process has such incredible zombie appeal.

4

McGOSPEL SALVATION
SO LIFELESS A DEAD MAN CAN DO IT
THE STICKY SWEET POISON OF EASY BELEIVISM

McGOSPEL SALVATION: SO LIFELESS A DEAD MAN CAN DO IT

THE STICKY SWEET POISON OF EASY BELIEVISM

"If you love soft preaching, you love a hard heart."

Doug Wilson

"Sermonettes make Christianettes."

A.W. Tozer

In November of 1970, George Harrison released the single *My Sweet Lord*, a folk rock tune that would rocket to the top of the international charts, all while proclaiming and exalting a love for the lord. For believers of many stripes, this was a beautiful thing. Even many Christians found Harrison's unexpected hymn to be appealing.

It sounded so good. It sounded so kind…so loving…so peaceful.

There was no questioning the song's sincerity; it was surely a song born of the heartfelt love of a man for his lord.

Early in the song, the Hebrew and Christian word for praise, hallelujah, can be heard permeating the chorus:

> *My sweet lord (hallelujah)*
> *Hm, my lord (hallelujah)*
> *My, my, my lord (hallelujah)*
> *Hmm (hallelujah)*

Then, as the soothing inspirational tune continues…

> *My sweet lord (hallelujah)*
> *My, my, lord (hallelujah)*
> *Hm, my lord (hare krishna)*
> *My, my, my lord (hare krishna)*
> *Oh hm, my sweet lord (krishna, krishna)*
> *Oh-uuh-uh (hare hare)*
> *Now, I really want to see you (hare rama)*
> *Really want to be with you (hare rama)*
> *Really want to see you lord (aaah)*
> *But it takes so long, my lord (hallelujah)*

In the span of the strum of a guitar in *My Sweet Lord*, the happy, probably-already-singing-along listener is treated to an unexpected revelation; a transformation from what was thought to be – and intentionally presented as – one thing, yet is revealed to be quite different.

And that intentional deception proved most significant in its impact.

In an interview with Harrison, scholar Mukunda Goswami observed, "I don't think it is possible to calculate just how many people were turned on to Krsna consciousness by your song *My Sweet Lord*."

Harrison's responded, "My idea in *My Sweet Lord*, because it sounded like a pop song, was to sneak up on them [the audience] a bit. The point was to have people not offended by 'Hallelujah', and by the time it gets to 'Hare Krsna' they're already hooked, and their foot's tapping and they're already singing along…to lull them into a sense of false security."

The guiding principle is clear: The ends justify the means, and the sweeter, more soothing, and peaceful seeming the means, the easier it becomes to guide a target toward an end that might have at one time seemed an impossible goal.

Few understand and share this appreciation for contorting and concealing substance in the name of pragmatism better than those driving the American Churchianity machine.

THE AMERICAN RELIGIOUS EMPIRE

"The Church has surrendered her once lofty concept of God and has substituted for it one so low, so ignoble, as to be utterly unworthy of thinking, worshiping men. This she has not done deliberately, but little by little and without her knowledge; and her very unawareness only makes her situation all the more tragic."

A.W. Tozer

"How could we have such a low view of the gospel of Jesus Christ that we have to manipulate men psychologically to get them to come down and pray a prayer? …How many times have I heard evangelists say, "It'll only take five minutes."? No my dear friend, it will take your life–all of it!"

Paul Washer

Where Harrison sought to blur and then obliterate the line between the Hindu god of Krishna and the Christian God Jesus, American Churchianity has a much easier time creating scores of seemingly viable bridges between the Christ of Christianity and the Flu Shot/Ripcord Jesus duo of modern American zombie religion, precisely because, by design, the counterfeits are thoroughly cloaked and covered in the language and terminology of the original which they seek to displace.

The name "Jesus" alone is enough to win over the more profoundly undiscerning – a group which, sadly, has come to represent a majority of professing evangelicals.

From there selectively added Bible terminology and vaguely Christian lingo is used to build, piece by piece, scores of secularly sound bridges between truth and lies, light and darkness, and life and death.

Any out-of-context verse/partial verse or concept that can be used to paint Jesus as a character defined almost exclusively by worldly definitions of love is eagerly employed for the sake of seeker sensitivity. And at the other end of the audience prep spectrum, anything that might be an "obstacle" to said seekers (such as the holy justice, wrath, jealousy, or anger of the Jesus of Scripture) is swept aside; completely removed as to allow for easy zombie shambling across the river Styx.

This careful, deliberate preparation is, in most cases, the result of many long hours, days, weeks, and even months of careful planning, staff meetings and strategy sessions. Books are written, bought, and read; conferences are planned, attended, and digested, and denominational growth strategies are conceived, formulated, and implemented – all for the purpose of cultivating ever better zombie herding techniques. Purpose-driven American Churchianity has become much more than a mere cottage industry; it is a modern religious/business empire. And this empire builds its future and its ranks ultimately through one all-important mechanism:

The altar call.

SETTING THE STAGE AND PREPPING THE MARKS

"Wherever pragmatism exits in the church, there is always a corresponding de-emphasis on Christ's sufficiency, God's sovereignty, biblical integrity, the power of prayer, and Spirit-led ministries. The result is a man-centered ministry that attempts to accomplish divine purposes by superficial programs and human methodology rather than by the Word or the power of the Spirit."

John MacArthur

So the mission is set. The church is prepared. Strategies are in place and it's time for the American Churchianity machine to roll into action.

The call goes out…

The Gospel call? No, not quite. This mission really doesn't call for or work particularly well with anything along the lines of, "God is holy, man is evil, and judgment is coming, so repent, believe and be saved!" Nope, that really doesn't fit here. It's *way* too much of a downer to be of much use to the purpose-driven business model at play here.

The call we're talking about here goes more like this:

We have a program for you!

…or…

We have a killer band for you!

…or…

We have a social setting for you!

…or…when all else fails…

We have pizza!

These are the sorts of evangelical calls that go out all across the nation each and every week thanks to the purpose-driven efforts of modern American Churchianity.

And while things like pizza, programs, bands, and social gatherings can be very good things, they are *not* the Gospel.

They are not close to the Gospel.

They are not even a part of the Gospel.

And that's precisely why they are used.

Like any good network marketer or pyramid scheme advocate, the wise American Churchianity religionist knows that the last thing you want to do in the process of courting a potential convert is tell them anything that might make them feel bad about anything – especially about themselves.

With that being Rule #1 in purpose-driven zombie evangelism, anything remotely resembling the true Gospel of Christ simply must go. It has no place.

Pizza, on the other hand…now that's a whole 'nother story.

This pizza-over-Gospel approach really does make perfect sense from a purpose-driven perspective. Remember: All unrepentant, rebellious men and women are born at war with God. They hate what He loves and love what He hates. They love the flesh and hate His Spirit. They are zombies.

Since the things that appeal to zombies are always distinct from the whole, undiluted Gospel of Jesus Christ, so too then must the evangelical call of American Churchianity also be clear in its separation from the whole, undiluted Gospel of Jesus Christ – at least if the church wishes to keep those numbers growing…and it does…above all else.

Numbers are the standard. Popularity the goal. Zombie-appeal is everything.

Church growth has become measured in entirely pagan terms. It's more than content with professions of faith (without expecting a changed life) and pledges of membership (without expecting regular attendance), so long as those precious, all-important numbers are there.

The ledger is everything.

Numbers are clearly one of the great idols of the present American church age.

Quantity has completely eclipsed quality in the purpose-driven, man-centered mind of American religious leadership, precisely because the quality standards associated with *actual* biblical evangelism and Christianity, as defined and explicitly recorded in Scripture, are quite literally unknown and unknowable to zombies – *all* zombies – be they in the streets, in the pews, or in leadership positions within the organizational machinery of American Christianity.

And make no mistake, zombies most certainly permeate all three locations – all by design and, in most cases, to the sheer joy of religious leaders.

After all, leadership has a vested interest in preserving the empire it worked so hard to build, and, in order to keep this train a-rolling, the flesh must be fed.

This sort of thing is nothing new; it's happened many times before. It's the norm in human history.

It's just what fallen men do.

It's the natural, predictable outcome of zombies playing religion.

From the first century Christian church to today, all zombie religion roads lead, in some form or fashion, to and through one place, conceptually if not literally.

That place is Rome.

WHEN IN ROME

> "All that we call human history--money, poverty, ambition, war, prostitution, classes, empires, slavery--[is] the long terrible story of man trying to find something other than God which will make him happy."
>
> C.S. Lewis, *Mere Christianity*

> "Man's nature, so to speak, is a perpetual factory of idols."
>
> John Calvin

Zombie religion is, has always been, and will always be, about man.

Man's desires, man's goals, man's concerns, man's needs, man's wants, man's rules, man's systems, man's standards...man, man, man. Ultimately, zombie religion aims to appease man's conscience by pleasing God just enough to gain His favor using man's standards of goodness through man-made systems and practices, commonly known as religion.

This was true when Jesus lived in Palestine during His earthly ministry and He made war on the dominant religion of the day. It was true when God raised the German Monk Martin Luther roughly 1,500 years later so that he might lead the Reformation against apostate religion that was dominating the world at that time. And it is most certainly true today in the age of American Churchianity.

Practically every protestant denomination in America has adopted a very *Roman* – in the Roman Catholic sense – notion of who God is, who man is, how salvation works, and what it produces when it does work.

And the supposed Protestants most likely to exhibit this modern day subliminal shift toward Romanism are the common folks who make up the bulk of most congregations – the moms, pops, and kids who occasionally warm the back pews and came in the first place for the programs, socializing, and pizza.

They are theologically casual at best. In large part because church leadership is more than happy to simply tell them what to think, as opposed to insisting that they learn how to search Scripture themselves.

They are practically indistinguishable from the world. This because, even if they've claimed membership and done the "get saved" thing, they are, in fact, unconverted. They live like the world, think like the world, love what the world loves, and hate what the world hates.

And they just *know* they're saved.

Why?

Because their church Father – I mean, *Pastor* – told them so. They barely, if ever, read their Bible, and feel no need to do so. They have little or no interest in right theology or doctrine. They are happy to go with the flow of the world. And they are depending on what their church father/pastor/system has told them in order to perpetuate the self-delusion of their own salvation.

It's hard to get more Roman than that.

And it is this very Roman environment that permeates every aspect of the American Churchianity presentation. Whether first or fiftieth time "visitor", the potential convert has the central tenants of this particular spin on zombie religion reinforced at every turn. The man-centeredness of it all is emphasized again and again as Flu Shot Jesus waits for his grand entry at the end of the show. Several critical elements of the pre-game show are perfected and deployed to aid in setting the seeker-sensitive stage, tone, and vibe, including:

- Zombies are to hear little or nothing the biblical concept of sin, much less the word itself. It might hurt their feelings, and we can't have that.
- Zombies are to be protected from the notion that Christianity actually requires anything measurable from them (other than "tithing", of course).
- Zombies are to be shown – ideally via colorful bulletin boards and posters – the plethora of wonderful programs, ministries, basketball leagues, pot lucks, fishing trips, BBQs, movie nights, summer camps, winter retreats, bowling leagues, hunting trips, breakfast groups, water park visits, hiking trips, reading groups, car clubs, financial seminars, and any number of other creative "need meeting" ideas dreamt up by the church staff, through which said zombies can entertain, satisfy, and/or distract themselves as they see fit.
- Zombies are to constantly have impressed upon them how easy it is to join the Christian club. They are to be asked important theological questions like "Got Jesus?" by way of t-shirt, poster, and bumper sticker at every opportunity.

With the seeker sensitive stage and mood set, it's showtime!
Ideally, an empathetic, charismatic pastor/preacher will present a touching, emotion-driven "sermon" dealing little with biblical truth in context and much with the felt needs of hard core Oprah and Dr. Phil fans. He/she will weave a tale that finally centers on how badly Jesus just wants to be allowed to give you everything that your little heart desires and if you'll just say yes to him, that's exactly what he'll do. Everything from financial peace to physical health to relationship restoration can be yours…

…but wait, there's more!

Much more!

The biggie – the one ginormous mega gift that this Jesus guy is just begging to give you – is the promise of a secure eternity. That's right, Heaven can be yours. And all you have to do is say one…little…prayer…

It'll just take two minutes, tops, so don't sweat it.

And you won't have to sweat anything after those two minutes are properly spent, so how can you resist?!

I mean, it's like: *Free Heaven!*

That one's pretty much a no-brainer for the garden variety American zombie.

So there you have it – another fish-in-the-barrel easy score for Pastor Feelgood and the McGospel Product of American Churchianity, another zombie expecting Heaven but destined for Hell, and another tallied member for the Church of the Living Dead.

SECTION 2

THE FLESH DRIVEN CHURCH OF THE LIVING DEAD

HOWLING WOLVES, BLOATED GOATS, AND STARVING SHEEP
McGOSPEL TRUTHS AND CONSEQUENCES

"And then she understood the devilish cunning of the enemies' plan. By mixing a little truth with it they had made their lie far stronger."

C.S. Lewis, *The Last Battle*

Pay careful attention to yourselves and to all the flock, in which the Holy Spirit has made you overseers, to care for the church of God, which he obtained with his own blood. I know that after my departure **fierce wolves will come in among you**, *not sparing the flock; and* **from among your own selves will arise men speaking twisted things, to draw away the disciples after them***. Therefore be alert, remembering that for three years I did not cease night or day to admonish everyone with tears.*

Acts 20:28-31 (Bold emphasis added)

It's not every day that you get the chance to watch your best friend nearly washed over the deck of a fishing boat in the middle of the Bering Sea, but there I was, at the age of nineteen, taking in just that sort of dramatic sight. Rustin and I had taken to the high seas for adventure and treasure, and this was what it had led to.

 The Norwegian boat owners of the *Pacific Orion* had quickly established a reputation for squeezing every dime's worth out of their crew, and since they were paying us a small (some would say large) fortune for our time, they had this annoying propensity to find "busy work" for us when the fishing was slow, we were sailing back to port, or something had broken in a way that prevented us from doing our normal jobs.

They were relentless in their commitment to have us doing something – anything – but sitting around during our scheduled "on time". We washed walls. We scrubbed floors. We even "cleaned" wooden pallets in the freezer hold with soy sauce – yes, *soy sauce* (there was a reason for this; a story for another time). I never saw so much Kikkoman…

Good times.

Over the first few weeks we were on board, these Scandinavian slave-drivers demonstrated a genuine creative talent for devising inane make-work projects. One can only assume that they are now employed in Washington DC.

At any rate, one of the more brilliant employee-squeezing assignments that was doled out came Rus' way when he was told to "mop the deck" while we were at sea. In very stormy weather. With big waves. Really. Big. Waves.

These really big waves were crashing right onto the deck that Rus was swabbing, and I was watching it all from the cozy interior of the getting-cleaner-by-the-minute *Pacific Orion*. There he was, yellow rain gear on (to match the yellow mop bucket/squeezer thingie), with his bucket rolling away from him as the boat listed in the crazy wavy water. And there I was, in sweats…probably with some hot cocoa.

I'd have probably been horrified if I could have just…stopped…laughing. But, man, you should have seen it! You'd understand. And seriously, if he'd have actually been swept over the side by one of the many life-threatening waves crashing on and around him, I would have been right there to jump in. I mean, if he wasn't around to finish mopping, those wacked out Norwegians might make *me* do it.

Sometimes we engage in what can be rightly described as "exercises in futility". Like mopping the deck of a boat as ginormous ocean waves crash onto your head.

Sometimes we do these things because greedy, power-trippy Norwegians make us do them, and, in a certain "I will suck it up and do what I must to get what I am here for" sense, that's cool.

Admirable even, I think.

What is *not* cool is when we do these things – when we take these sorts of excessively dangerous risks – without any hope of the benefit we may associate with them actually being real. And that is precisely the situation in which we find the millions upon millions of zombies held under the sway of American Churchianity.

They believe that they are Heaven bound when they are actually on the *Highway to Hell*.

GIVING GOD THE FINGER... IN SONG

*I appeal to you, brothers, to watch out for those who cause divisions and create obstacles **contrary to the doctrine that you have been taught**; avoid them. For such persons do not serve our Lord Christ, but their own appetites, and by smooth talk and flattery they deceive the hearts of the naive.*

Romans 16:17-18 (Bold emphasis added)

"Heaven is full of forgiven people. Hell is full of forgiven people. Heaven is full of people God loves, whom Jesus died for. Hell is full of forgiven people God loves, whom Jesus died for. The difference is how we choose to live, which story we choose to live in, which version of reality we trust. Ours or God's."

Rob Bell, *Velvet Elvis* (page 146)

American Churchianity has left no road untraveled where the pursuit of the dead is concerned, and that includes AC/DC's *Highway to Hell*, which was performed as a part of "worship service" at the very same North Point Church that was chronicled in *Firing Breathing Christians* as having created and made available for sale in its bookstore the infamous *Girls Gone Wild, Bible Style* CD set. With a trajectory like this, one can only cringe at the "worship" possibilities that might spew forth from North Point Church in the coming years. In the meantime, for those of you unfamiliar with Highway to Hell, here are the lyrics, **as sung on stage at North Point in Jesus' name**:

Living easy, living free
Season ticket on a one-way ride
Asking nothing, leave me be
Taking everything in my stride
Don't need reason, don't need rhyme
Ain't nothing I would rather do
Going down, party time
My friends are gonna be there too
I'm on the highway to hell
No stop signs, speed limit
Nobody's gonna slow me down
Like a wheel, gonna spin it
Nobody's gonna mess me round
Hey Satan, payed my dues
Playing in a rocking band
Hey Momma, look at me
I'm on my way to the promised land
I'm on the highway to hell
(Don't stop me)
And I'm going down, all the way down
I'm on the highway to hell

Neat, huh?

Nothing says "I love Jesus" like a little *Highway to Hell* action. Or *Sympathy for the Devil* action (which the North Point Worship Team also cranked out and proudly promoted via YouTube).

Yessiree, North Point Church is on the cutting edge of…feeding the flesh.

And the zombies eat this stuff up.

North Point has become wildly popular and, by American Churchianity standards of measurement, "successful". And all it took was a few little seeker sensitive tidbits like Highway to Hell, Sympathy for the Devil, and Girls Gone Wild, Bible Style.

Clearly, there is no limit or floor or depth limiting these folks. Every option is on the table, and the zombies are lovin' it. Once this path was started, the possibilities became quite literally unlimited.

Just think about it for a moment; think about how they might try to "reach out" to, say, those who are into pornography, for example.

Okay, stop thinking about that.

Right now.

Those thoughts are dangerous when they wander…and when they are promoted on stage for hours on end at a "church".

This is where we are at. In rural, heartland America. In the Bible Belt Buckle. In an evangelical Church.

This is what has been explicitly attached to the name and honor of Jesus Christ.

Is the concept of "righteous anger" crystalizing in your mind right about now?

If so, good.

If not, exactly what *are* you smoking? (Not that anyone at North Point Church would care…)

THE OTHER HIGHWAY TO (NO) HELL

"As soon as the door is opened to Muslims. Hindus, Buddhists, and Baptists from Cleveland, many Christians become very uneasy, saying that then Jesus doesn't matter anymore, the cross is irrelevant, it doesn't matter what you believe, and so forth. Not true. Absolutely, unequivocally, unalterably not true. What Jesus does is declare that he, and he alone, is saving everybody."

Rob Bell, *Love Wins*

"There are those who hate Christianity and call their hatred an all-embracing love for all religions."

G.K. Chesterton

But even if we or an angel from heaven should preach to you a gospel contrary to the one we preached to you, let him be accursed. As we have said before, so now I say again: If anyone is preaching to you a gospel contrary to the one you received, let him be accursed.

For am I now seeking the approval of man, or of God? Or am I trying to please man? **If I were still trying to please man, I would not be a servant of Christ**.

Galatians 1:8-10 (Bold emphasis added)

So we've got Rob Bell denying Hell on one front, North Point Church singing about taking a highway there during "worship" services on another, and, if that wasn't enough, we are also graced with the Joel Osteens and Tyler Padgitts of the world who, at best, "just don't know" much about anything where things like our holy God's righteous anger, coming judgment, and eternal punishment for unrepentant *people* are concerned. In this, if we'll just open our eyes and ears, we are graciously presented with a solid look into the preferred leadership qualities in the world of American Churchianity, namely:

- An obsession with keeping zombies from discomfort.
- Irreverence for Scripture bordering on, and often crossing into, open hostility.
- A persona largely defined by false humility, and the use of this false humility as justification for avoiding harsh scriptural truths.
- An utter disinterest (again, bordering on contempt) for basic biblical concepts such as church discipline and purity.

Remember: These are popular "pastors" and teachers within the professing evangelical Christian community in America. This is where we are at in most of American Churchianity. And under the watchful eye and careful, deliberate guidance of these fine leaders, two groups have been radically impacted…in radically opposing ways.

The two groups in question are actual Christians, often described as "sheep" in Scripture, and all unconverted people, described in this book as zombies, and often in the Bible as "goats". When subjected to zombie religion leadership, the sheep are neglected, ridiculed, and oppressed, while goats grow are comforted, praised, and encouraged (to go right on being goats).

As we've gotten a glimpse of with "God isn't mad at anyone" themed sermons, "I don't know" if Jesus is the only way testimonials, and Highway to Hell/Sympathy for the Devil worship sessions, the driving force motivating American Churchianity is the feeding of what the Bible calls goats and the starving of what the Bible calls sheep. Put another way, American Churchianity is all about winning and maintaining zombie approval by feeding the flesh.

STARVING THE SHEEP

> *For an overseer, as God's steward, must be above reproach. He must not be arrogant or quick-tempered or a drunkard or violent or greedy for gain, but hospitable, a lover of good, self-controlled, upright, holy, and disciplined. He must hold firm to the trustworthy word as taught,* **so that he may be able to give instruction in sound doctrine and also to rebuke those who contradict it.**
>
> Titus 1:7-9 (Bold emphasis added)

"We fear men so much, because we fear God so little. One fear cures another. When man's terror scares you, turn your thoughts to the wrath of God."

William Gurnall

Sheep don't thrive on goat food, spiritually speaking. This being the case, sheep who find themselves in a goat-food heavy/sheep-food light environment, are destined to endure the following:

- **Neglect** – While the "felt needs" of zombies/goats will be sought out and met, the spiritual needs of "new creatures" in Christ will be ignored, if they're even recognized, by American Churchianity leadership.

- **Stagnation** – The *actual* Christian's growth will be inhibited, if not obstructed completely, through the deliberately shallow, "milk-only" (at best) spiritual diet plan implemented by the average contemporary Pastor Feelgood type.

- **Ridicule/Hostility** – Goats, be they in pulpit/leadership positions or entry level membership roles, inherently dislike sheep and will act accordingly.

- **Rejection/Ejection** – Sheep who don't "get with the purpose-driven program" and persist in advocating biblically sound practice in American Churchianity institutions – however gently or respectfully they may do so – will be strongly encouraged to leave via isolation and more open forms of hostility.

Remember: These consequences are anything *but* accidental. Christ's sheep are, have always been, and will always be acceptable – encouraged even – casualties of war when the battle in question involves the pursuit of the affections of the dead. This is all by purpose-driven, seeker-sensitive design…

…and the zombies are *lovin'* it.

FEEDING THE FLESH

For, speaking loud boasts of folly, they entice by sensual passions of the flesh those who are barely escaping from those who live in error.

2 Peter 2:18

"I hate preaching that goes something like this: 'You know, you've got a wonderful life there, yuppie. You've got a really nice house and a really nice job. You've got a beautiful wife and you've got 1.25 children and you've got three cars . . . You've got a great job. You've got a great life. Everything fits perfectly in place. You just lack one thing. You lack Jesus.' That is the most disgusting thing you could ever say. What would be more appropriate to say is, 'Sir, your life is nothing. It has no value at all apart from Jesus Christ.' He is not some accessory that a yuppie puts on top of his life as though it were a cherry on top of ice cream."

Paul Washer

And how do those living dead, known as goats, fare when the American Churchianity machine is running smoothly and hitting on all purpose-driven cylinders? Well, as you probably surmised, they experience precisely the opposite of what actual Christians (sheep) are subjected to, including:

- **Adoration** – The goats are made to feel comfortable and welcome in every way possible. American Churchianity is

- all about man, with man being defined as the lost in rebellion, so it is that American Churchianity is all about *them* – the goats.

- **Affirmation** – The desires, hopes, and needs of the flesh are often encouraged as natural (which they are, for a zombie) and good (which they are not, as a holy God defines "good").

- **Inoculation** – Through scores of thoroughly religious machinations, and with just enough "Jesus lingo" sprinkled on top to make them convinced of this religion's "Christianity", zombies are effectively inoculated against the true Gospel of Christ.

A fine test of the truth of that last statement can be readily performed in the South – "Bible Country".

So thoroughly has American Churchianity perversion swept through our culture that, if you approach an obvious false convert – one who has made a profession of faith for years yet shows absolutely nothing of the biblically prescribed fruit of their "conversion" – and you begin to share the Gospel with them, they are quite likely to respond with something like, as Paul Washer has described, "Don't worry about me; I done did that".

The "that" in question is "get saved", of course, and the "done did" is code for "I said a prayer" or "I made a profession" or "I walked an aisle" or…you get the picture.

This is the spiritual wasteland created by apostate Christianity in America. While many professing evangelicals enjoy painting places like San Francisco, New York City, and Seattle as front-line spiritual battlegrounds – strongholds of secularism, if you will – it is, in fact, the "evangelical South" that has become the most entrenched anti-Christian region in the nation. With millions upon millions of zombies who are, thanks to Pastor Feelgood and his All-American Salvation Machine, utterly convinced of their salvation still quite dead and roaming the southern countryside and cities, what was once the geographic springboard for biblical evangelism in America and the world has now become the part of the nation most in need of – and hardened against – the whole, undiluted, supernatural Gospel of Christ.

All thanks to American Churchianity.

And all in Jesus' name, of course.

FOLLOW THE ZOMBIE MONEY

And others are the ones sown among thorns. They are those who hear the word, but the cares of the world and the deceitfulness of riches and the desires for other things enter in and choke the word, and it proves unfruitful.

Mark 4:18-19

For the love of money is a root of all kinds of evils. It is through this craving that some have wandered away from the faith and pierced themselves with many pangs.

1 Timothy 6:10

If the tag line for Romero's *Dawn of the Dead* was, "When there's no more room in Hell, the dead will walk the earth", then an appropriate promo for the pragmatic, zombie-friendly, bottom-line approach of American Churchianity could easily read: "When there's no more room in Hell…it's time for another building fund!"

And in this we see a direct path to the strange sort of simultaneous slavery that American Churchianity has to the zombies and the zombies have to American Churchianity. The ramping-up process to this mutual slavery situation goes something like this:

1. A "church" attracts zombies with flashy building additions/expansions that cost a lot of money – usually money acquired by going into debt.

2. Said "church" succeeds in attracting zombies and also succeeds in convincing these inherently undiscerning folks that "tithing" is still in effect (and is, ironically, the only rule really emphasized where the "Christian walk" is concerned).

3. Zombies tithe.

4. The "church" is then, through financial dependence, effectively controlled by the zombies.

Neat, huh?
See how easy, and predictable that was?
And what do zombies want in their newly acquired "church"?
Why, they want their flesh fed, of course!
They want entertainment.
And in American Churchianity, zombies get what zombies want.

6

SIX FLAGS OVER JESUS
THE MALL OF AMERICAN CHURCHIANITY

SIX FLAGS OVER JESUS
THE MALL OF AMERICAN CHURCHIANITY

"The person who loves you most will tell you the most truth. One of the greatest distinguishing marks of a false prophet is that he will always tell you what you want to hear, he will never rain on your parade, he will get you clapping, he will get you jumping, he will make you dizzy, he will keep you entertained, and he will present a Christianity to you that will make your church look like a Six Flags over Jesus. And keep you so entertained you are never addressed with great issues such as these:

Is God working in my life?
Am I growing in holiness?
Have I truly been born again?"

Paul Washer

"For where God built a church, there the Devil would also build a chapel."

Martin Luther

Hell on earth had come. The apocalypse was upon them. But they had found relief. They had found happiness. They had found joy.

They had found...*a shopping mall.*

And it was theirs...*all theirs.*

There were shoes, books, boots, toys, shirts, games, pants, hats, televisions, toys, coats...the list of treasures went on and on. They presented themselves infinite variety and, best of all, they were freely available, without cost to eager consumers. As their eyes struggled to stay wide to take it all in and their hearts surged with anticipation of the desires about to be indulged, the beauty of it all nearly overwhelmed them. It was amazing, and almost unbelievably so –the classic "too good to be true" scenario come to life amidst the death that surrounded this island oasis in a sea of death – a death that would inevitably claim them, but, until it did, they had found every*thing* that they had ever wanted.

Right there in the mall.

Of all of the social commentaries made throughout George Romero's series of zombie films, perhaps the most enduring illustration came through his use of a shopping mall as the setting of 1978s *Dawn of the Dead*. In this first sequel to *Night of the Living Dead*, four survivors of the zombie outbreak manage to escape to a shopping mall, where they attempt to hole up, distract themselves with every material thing their hearts desire, and ride out the apocalypse in style.

THE MALL OF AMERICAN CHURCHIANITY

"The Lord commonly gives riches to foolish people, to whom he gives nothing else."

Martin Luther

"No one is so miserable as the poor person who maintains the appearance of wealth."

Charles Spurgeon

For every ministry in American Churchianity clearly dedicated to aiding Christian parents in honoring their obligation to God to personally raise and instruct their children in righteousness, there are roughly 3.2 gajillion other, less-biblical "ministries" implemented in the form of book stores, coffee shops, drum kits, puppet shows, exercise rooms, and basketball courts "on campus". Apparently raising one's children properly (as Christ defines these terms) doesn't make the "felt needs of zombies" list. Hence, such biblical ministries are about as common as a happy ending in a Romero flick.

But coffee bars? Check.

Ditto for bookstores. And workout rooms. And club-style stages with cool lights. If there's a need being felt out there in the blackened little hearts of the dead, there's a corresponding product to be found at The Mall of American Churchianity.

Flesh is well fed here. 24/7, seven days a week, and twice on Sunday.

We built it. And they came. Right on cue and just as we'd hoped.

They came for the programs, products, and presentations aimed at comforting and encouraging the unrepentant dead. As the zombie hordes flocked to these enticements, the need for their expansion became apparent. Zombies tend to bore quickly, so the impulse to perpetually multiply and amplify the entertainment was automatic, irresistible, and all-consuming.

In order to maintain the attention and devotion of those lured through secular appeal, the same secular appetites must perpetually be fed. And as those appetites perpetually increase as they are fed, this endlessly escalating chase is inevitably catastrophic in nature. It never ends well. George Romero seems to know this all too well; Joel Osteen, not so much.

Entertaining the dead can be quite expensive, both figuratively and literally. Coffee bars, book stores, basketball courts and the like cost money. Lots of money. On the plus side, zombies have money, so the American Churchianity experience is, in at least one sense, a match made in Heaven…or that other place Rob Bell likes to dismiss.

SLAVES OF THE DEAD

…the borrower is the slave of the lender.

Proverbs 22:7

"The God of this world is riches, pleasure and pride."

Martin Luther

"The free will is a pagan goddess that the Church has worshipped for far too long."

Steve Lawson

Early on in *Dawn of the Dead*, Peter, one of the four survivors at the heart of the story, relays a theory as to why the nightmare scenario that they were enduring had come to pass by observing, "Something my granddad used to tell us. You know Macumba? Voodoo. My granddad was a priest in Trinidad. He used to tell us, 'When there's no more room in hell, the dead will walk the earth.'" In modern American Churchianity, the formula seems to be, "When there's no more room in Hell's staging ground, it's time for another building fund!"

With this approach embraced, fund after fund for addition after addition comes and goes, one giving way to the next, each bringing with it a new mountain of debt through which the "church" in question is then, in effect, enslaved to the unrepentant dead that then dominate its membership.

Philosophical enslavement of a church to the dead is then further entrenched through this financial indebtedness, and the already dim prospects for the promotion of biblical models of worship and church activity become even more encumbered.

The situation is as easy to understand as it is pathetic in nature:

1. The church attracts customers (zombies/goats) via flesh feeding, seeker-sensitive accessories.
2. The provision of these accessories leads a church into financial debt.
3. The zombies then demand ever-increasing amounts and varieties of said accessories, which require ever-increasing amounts of financial debt.
4. Zombies then effectively rule the church, having enslaved it to their appetite for flesh by enslaving it to the debt required on the part of the church to feed that appetite.

This more detailed spin on the list presented in Chapter 5 presents a more clear backdrop against which we can see the true desperation of the situation from the perspective of any pastor who may, upon finding himself in the position of leading such a church, find it impossible to risk the financial collapse of his church by doing or saying anything that might drive those precious "tithing" zombies away.

It is this slippery slope that has ensnared and subsequently defined much of the American Churchianity Empire…one coffee bar at a time.

Casualties of Churchianity

For which of you, desiring to build a tower, does not first sit down and count the cost, whether he has enough to complete it? Otherwise, when he has laid a foundation and is not able to finish, all who see it begin to mock him, saying, 'This man began to build and was not able to finish.'

Luke 14:28-30

"We have come to a turning point in the road. If we turn to the right mayhap our children and our children's children will go that way; but if we turn to the left, generations yet unborn will curse our names for having been unfaithful to God and to His Word."

Charles Spurgeon

It is this preoccupation with the flesh that has made it utterly impossible – at least financially from a secular perspective – for churches in this mold to make any time, or money, for biblically prescribed ministries.

The financial debt accrued in the pursuit of the dead has made finding money for biblical ministries impossible, and the philosophical debt accrued through the acquisition of a zombie-dominated congregation makes finding the courage to even speak of such ministries openly and clearly nearly impossible. After all, we don't dare offend the zombies who are paying our second (and third, and fourth) mortgages, now do we?

So it is that young fathers and mothers in the church are not provided with biblical ministries aimed squarely at helping them to better assume and fulfill their biblically prescribed roles and responsibilities as fathers and mothers, children do not benefit from the biblically prescribed homes that would result from said ministries, and the chain of secularly defined family and home concepts goes on, unbroken by biblical truth. All for the sake of zombie comfort. And all in Jesus' name.

The Mall of American Churchianity is every bit the zombie magnet that was the shopping mall in Romero's *Dawn of the Dead*. And it is infinitely more offensive to the Jesus in whose name it was built.

7

THE CORROSIVE CHARACTER OF
CANDY CHRISTIANITY
THE ANTI-CHRISTIAN PRODUCT OF AN ANTI-CHRISTIAN GOSPEL

THE CORROSIVE CHARACTER OF CANDY CHRISTIANITY

THE ANTI-CHRISTIAN PRODUCT OF AN ANTI-CHRISTIAN GOSPEL

"The world's theology is easy to define. It is the view that human beings are basically good, that no one is really lost, that belief in Jesus Christ is not necessary for salvation."

James Montgomery Boice

"Fallacies do not cease to be fallacies because they become fashions."

G.K. Chesterton

In the mid-'80s, I attended what we Southern Baptists in the Twin Lakes region of North-central Arkansas at the time referred to as a "youth rally". I was just heading into my teen years and had been active at Henderson First Baptist Church since Gram started bringing me there a few years earlier.

The youth rally concept was simple enough – gather a bunch of kids from member churches throughout the region once a month to meet, socialize and, ideally, somewhere over the course of an evening, learn something. Even more ideally, learn something *good*.

The subject of this particular rally was the dangers of rock 'n' roll.

I hadn't really been all that impressed with rock heading into the event; I was much more of a science-fiction and fantasy geek. While I had a thing for Led Zeppelin and Elvis, I definitely preferred Star Wars and monster movies to star guitarists and monsters of rock.

There were hundreds of kids packed into a little white church just off the highway; all gathered 'round the image being projected onto a wall in the small building's sanctuary. And there on the screen, for the first time that I remember, I was introduced to Twisted Sister's Dee Snider. I might have seen him peripherally before; it's hard to say since he and his band were pretty much *everywhere* on the pop culture scene those days. What struck me was his over-the-top persona and appearance. Let's just say it was very "monster movie"…very "fantastic"…I saw much more Dracula or Frankenstein in Snider's costume than anything "gender bending" or "lady like", which seemed to be the main gripe of the anti-rock documentary's narrator.

And that Monster Persona thing, for me, seemed kinda cool. I mean, the guy looked ridiculous, but in such an over-the-top, hyper-dramatic way, that it was impossible for me to view him as anything but funny in a cool kind of way. The main criticism sent Dee's way regarding his appearance as the evils of Twisted Sister and their ilk were chronicled in the video production for the assembled Southern Baptist kiddos was that he was some sort of cross-dresser; that he was trying to look like a woman or something.

Now, make no mistake, Twisted Sister as a band and Dee Snider in particular was definitely heavy on the make-up and what would normally be described as "women's garb" as a part of the whole "twisted" persona, but if there was one thing that these guys were *not*, it was feminine. My sense was then as it is now: Dee Snider, when in full blown "Twisted Sister mode", is quite possibly the least feminine, the least lady-like, and the least likely to be mistaken for a woman human being in all of recorded (and unrecorded) history.

As the Snider/Sister clip rolled and the documentary's narrator expressed grave concern that Mr. Snider was leading the culture in a gender bending direction by way of his feminine and womanly appearance, I was horrified. Not at Dee, but at the narrator's notion of things like "womanly" and "feminine". I mean, Twisted Sister...*womanly?* All I knew for sure was that, if Snider struck this narrator as even *vaguely* feminine in appearance, I definitely *didn't* want to see a picture of is wife or daughter.

In Snider, I saw much more of a Dracula or Frankenstein figure than a Boy George type. Then, as I was still soaking in the narrator's disconnect with reality where the feminine look was concerned, the next hit came when the video played through some of Twisted Sister's *I Wanna Rock*.

I liked it. A lot.

And within a month, I'd bought my first two rock and roll LPs: Twisted Sister's *Stay Hungry* and another featured target of the youth rally video, Quiet Riot's *Metal Health*.

Nice job, Twin Lakes Baptists. Way to make an impact.

By the grace of God, I never really got into anything like a "rock 'n' roll" lifestyle, though I was a fan of the music. In the '80s, I continued to follow some of those bands originally discovered at the Southern Baptist event, including Quiet Riot.

About a decade after *Metal Health* and "the youth rally", and after I'd already hit the high seas of adventure in Alaska, I had the opportunity to catch Quiet Riot perform in Little Rock at a club called Juanita's Cantina. Clearly, QR's star had faded, what with the former stadium headliners now playing in a club for a couple hundred Little Rockers, but I was still jazzed to see 'em.

After the show, I had the opportunity to talk a while with the band's lead singer and star, Kevin DuBrow. As I was probably one of only two people in the crowd (the other being my friend, Rus) who watched the show but didn't drink, I was able to have and interested in having an actual, coherent conversation with this guy who'd made something of an impact on me when I was younger, more impressionable, and more inclined toward involvement with Southern Baptist youth groups. And Kevin, to his credit, was happy to oblige.

He was kind, articulate, and attentive enough to my thoughts and questions. He seemed like a nice enough, if profoundly confused, guy.

And I never once shared the Gospel with him.

Pathetic.

Or maybe not…I mean, maybe he was just a "carnal Christian", right?

Anything Goes in Zombieland

"The preacher is not a chef; he's a waiter. God doesn't want you to make the meal; He just wants you to deliver it to the table without messing it up. That's all."

John MacArthur

"If you love me, you will keep my commandments."

Jesus (The Real One) in John 14:15

Over the years that followed the Juanita's appearance, '80s heavy metal and Quiet Riot in particular enjoyed something of a resurgence. DuBrow and company were able to continue to rock, roll, and the other things that tend to go along with the first two. The band regained some momentum and what the world would easily regard as positive trajectory (meaning: material success). Things were rolling along quite nicely, all things considered, at least from a secular perspective.

Then, in November of 2007, DuBrow was found dead in his home. The cause of death was listed as an accidental cocaine overdose.

After a life of rock and roll "glory", one man's eternity unexpectedly began in November of 2007. So he's a few years into forever…

Now, if that man was said to have been involved in all of the indulgences that one associates with a rocker's lifestyle – drugs, promiscuity, etc. – and he comes to a cocaine fueled end, one might use his story as a cautionary tale built upon the assumed, if unspoken or declared, proposition that such a man was surely now committed to an eternal fate defined by unmitigated exposure to the pure wrath of a holy God.

But consider this: What if I told you that this man had, at one time in his past – perhaps as a boy – made a profession of faith, walked the aisle, said the prayer, and proclaimed publically Jesus as his savior. What then? Would we view his profession, prayer, and walk down the aisle as having actually been enough to save him?

In American Churchianity, the answer is a loud and clear *yes*.

In American Churchianity, the profession is everything. That's just how Flu Shot Jesus works. It's who he is.

In American Churchianity, you can do *anything* and still be considered "in", so long as you jump through a few simple religious hoops. And that'll take only five minutes, tops.

It's like the indulgences sold by the "church" in the good old days, only much cheaper. Instead of gold, you just pay with a few words and maybe a walk down an aisle. You can love the world in practice while claiming Christ with words. You can freely feed your flesh while lip-synching a love for the Lord.

Talk about a *very* marketable gospel! What's not for a zombie to like here? I mean, you can have your flesh and feed it, too.

This is what the happy land of seeker-sensitivity calls "carnal Christianity".

In a nutshell, it simply means that you can do whatever you want while maintaining what the American "church" considers a credible claim to Christ as savior.

You can even record a cover of *Highway to Hell*, just as DuBrow and QR did. After all, as we've already covered ourselves, North Point Church's house "worship" band has done the same.

Anything goes.

You can blaze a trail through life that'd make Caligula blush, and do it with full assurance from American Churchianity that you are, at the end of that wild and rockin' road, safely and securely Heaven bound. It's all good…and carnal…so long as you sign off at some point "in Jesus' name."

THE CORROSIVE CHARACTER OF CANDY CHRISTIANITY

POST-CHRISTIAN AMERICAN "CHRISTIANS"

*If we say that we have fellowship with Him and yet walk in the darkness, we **lie** and do not practice the truth*

           1 John 1:6 (NASB – Bold emphasis added)

"Of two evils, choose neither."

           Charles Spurgeon

"Most Americans believe they, themselves, will go to heaven. Yet, when asked to describe their views about the religious destiny of others, people become much less forgiving." So begins an April, 2011 Barna Group report entitled *What Americans Believe About Universalism and Pluralism*. The report provided some insight into the state of American Churchianity when it came to addressing how "Christian" Americans answered some critical questions on issues central to an orthodox Christian understanding or worldview:

> "When looking at the Christian community, born again Christians were more likely to be interested in sharing their faith with others as well as more likely than average to say they desire active, healthy relationships with people of other faiths. [Born again Christians are defined by Barna Group as those who have made a commitment to Jesus Christ and who believe they are going to heaven because of their confession of sins and accepted Christ as

their savior. It is not based upon self-identifying with the label "born again."]

Nevertheless, despite their own personal faith convictions, many born again Christians embrace certain aspects of universalist thought. One-quarter of born again Christians said that all people are eventually saved or accepted by God (25%) and that it doesn't matter what religious faith you follow because they all teach the same lessons (26%). An even larger percentage of born again Christians (40%) indicated that they believe Christians and Muslims worship the same God."

Somewhere, Rob Bell is smiling. Pro'ly giggling, too. And yeah, that tends to be a bad thing.

Universalism is a natural consequence of three major themes permeating American religion over the past century, with one building into the next:

1. A lethargy/disinterest regarding the pursuit of biblical truth.

2. A general disinterest in the pursuit of deep truth through Scripture naturally produced shallow, unbiblical theologies and dogmas built largely upon the exaltation of man and man's happiness as the center of God's plan and focus of His attention.

3. The sovereignty of man in salvation. The exaltation of man over God in the single most important area of any man's life is precisely what one would expect when one holds to an anthropocentric (man centered) rather than a theocentric (God centered) theology.

When man's standards of fairness and morality are applied to a perfect, holy God – the Author of morality and truth – we are quite obviously on a very slippery slope to nowhere good, and when we add an American flavor to the context, the attraction to an "every man gets a vote" or "every man has a shot" philosophy is quite reasonable.

Reasonable by the standards of a self-referential rebel, that is, which is another way of saying: completely wrong.

THE ALL-AMERICAN SOVEREIGNTY OF MAN

"The free will is a pagan goddess that the Church has worshipped for far too long."

Steve Lawson

"The plot has been lost, and it's time to reclaim it.

A staggering number of people have been taught that a select few Christians will spend forever in a peaceful, joyous place called heaven, while the rest of humanity spends forever in torment and punishment in hell with no chance for anything better.... This is misguided and toxic and ultimately subverts the contagious spread of Jesus' message of love, peace, forgiveness, and joy that our world desperately needs to hear."

Rob Bell, *Love Wins*

"Farewell, Rob Bell."

John Piper, via Twitter in response to *Love Wins*

Rob Bell, for example (and he is but one of many), when he denies the orthodox Christian understanding of everything from the nature of man to the existence of an eternal Hell, is merely carrying Arminian theology to a very logical conclusion. And while we're talking theology, two things to note about the "Arminian" strain:

- The vast majority of American evangelicals have no idea what Arminian theology is.
- The vast majority of American evangelicals nonetheless subscribe to Arminian theology.

Arminianism – the well-established, cherished, and vigorously defended norm in modern American Churchianity – is named for Dutch theologian Jacobus Arminius (1560-1609) and holds that Christ atoned for all sins of all men and that this atonement is limited not by God's will and purpose, but by man's.

It is this view of soteriology and its inevitable impact on one's understanding of the nature of God, man, and holiness that has come to define virtually every aspect of modern American religion and theology. And when we consider that, as many good, God-fearing men have noted, most heresies and/or cultish systems of belief find their root in a fundamental misunderstanding as to the nature of God, we see in the embrace of Arminianism the origin of much of what has corrupted the American church.

A reverence for the true nature of God is indeed the foundation of all good and accurate knowledge, wisdom, and understanding. The essential nature of this "starting point" is made plain throughout the pages of Scripture:

> *The fear of the LORD is the beginning of wisdom, and the knowledge of the Holy One is insight.* – Proverbs 9:10

> *The fear of the LORD is the beginning of knowledge; fools despise wisdom and instruction.* – Proverbs 1:7

THE CORROSIVE CHARACTER OF CANDY CHRISTIANITY

The fear of the LORD is the beginning of wisdom; all those who practice it have a good understanding. His praise endures forever! – Psalm 111:10

While the temptation is great to critique the decline of American Christianity into American Churchianity by focusing on the effects or symptoms (universalism, self-referential morality, postmodern thought, etc.) rather than the cause (an ignorance/abandonment of the true nature of God as the foundation for knowledge), it is vital that we not skip over the problem's taproot in order to merely prune its leaves, however preferable that pruning might seem.

It is only when we see clearly that all true knowledge and wisdom really does begin with the nature of God – and a right understanding thereof – that we will begin to understand how and why seeker-sensitive, purpose-driven paths have become so prevalent. When we see that the God-centered worldview that permeated the American spirit, consciousness and theology of the revolutionary era has been systematically replaced by a man-centered spirit and theology today, we will have far less trouble understanding why things have fallen into the horrible state in which we find them today. We will finally stop asking, "How could this happen?" and start understanding that, once we jettisoned a theocentric worldview for an anthropocentric one, our current condition became inevitable.

We will also understand that, if this situation is not corrected, our culture's trajectory will not change. And without that change, far darker consequences are every bit as inevitable as any which we have endured to this point.

On that happy note, let's have a look at what the man-centered Candy Christianity defining modern American religion has wrought through example, instruction, and tradition...

WHEN SELF-LOVE WINS

But understand this, that in the last days there will come times of difficulty. For people will be lovers of self, lovers of money, proud, arrogant, abusive, disobedient to their parents, ungrateful, unholy, heartless, unappeasable, slanderous, without self-control, brutal, not loving good, treacherous, reckless, swollen with conceit, lovers of pleasure rather than lovers of God, having the appearance of godliness, but denying its power. Avoid such people.

2 Timothy 3:1-5

"Reason is a whore, the greatest enemy that faith has."

Martin Luther

Through seeker-sensitive and purpose-driven models and methods, much of the professing church in America has been conformed to the world that she was commissioned to transform, and as her apostasy has solidified, she has become a conduit for the rot that has corrupted her. She processes everything through a man-centered filter and passes along various strains and interpretations of this fundamental (and deliberate) error to her followers through scores of practices, which eventually mutate into human traditions. And in an age of biblical illiteracy combined with bold historical ignorance, tradition has become the primary guiding force for most professing evangelicals in modern American Churchianity – just as it was in the Roman religion at the time of the Protestant Reformation.

THE CORROSIVE CHARACTER OF CANDY CHRISTIANITY

Consider the following "lessons" taught implicitly through the deliberate, methodical practices that permeate modern American Churchianity:

- Man is sovereign over the matter most important to him – his salvation. This placing of man on God's throne in "just one" area (not coincidentally, the most important area from the man's perspective) is the core of zombie religion. This "I will determine my own fate" is also the core of satanic thought.

- Debt is good…so long as you're using it to build something with serious zombie appeal, like a coffee shop or basketball court.

- The purity of the Bride of Christ is insignificant. For the vast majority of seeker-sensitive churches, biblical church discipline is not only dismissed, but openly ridiculed because it is – you guessed it – not popular with "seekers" (aka "zombies").

When we consider just these three significant repudiations of clear biblical truth on the part of American Churchianity in practice, we more clearly see the bridge that's been built between a refusal to embrace a fear and reverence for the Lord as He has revealed Himself in His perfect Word, and the moral and economic depravity that now defines American culture.

Through our abandonment of "the fear of the Lord" in favor of Candy Christianity, we've embraced a path that inevitably leads to where we are now…a path that continues on to much lower places…a path that is paved by one of the most powerful forces in human history:

Tradition.

The slavery of modern American religion to the force of human tradition has been forged over many decades' time. Many professing and actual Christians - even those in their later years – have literally known nothing but this recent aberration that calls itself Christianity in America. They've never known anything but a submissive Jesus. They've never known anything but control - or sovereignty...or Lordship – over their own salvation. They've never known a world or a God that isn't preoccupied with *their* happiness and *their* comfort.

They are so blinded by these man-made, man-centered traditions that they are unable to even see, much less resist them. Tradition defines their theology. Tradition paves their path to all things.

And this road, as all others in the man-centered mold, leads to Rome.

As the twelve-steppers like to say, the first step to solving a problem is admitting that it exists. Identification is the key. Only with the origin of our cultural – and individual – predicament identified are we able to begin to chart a path toward something better...something true...something good...

Only through the embrace of a true, biblical "fear of the Lord", and the supernatural power that follows, can we hope to save a dead nation and culture...one zombie at a time...

SECTION

3

THE RAZING OF HELL

RAISING THE DEAD

THE SUPERNATURAL POWER OF THE SUPERNATURAL GOSPEL

Then Jesus, deeply moved again, came to the tomb. It was a cave, and a stone lay against it. Jesus said, "Take away the stone." Martha, the sister of the dead man, said to him, "Lord, by this time there will be an odor, for he has been dead four days." Jesus said to her, "Did I not tell you that if you believed you would see the glory of God?" So they took away the stone. And Jesus lifted up his eyes and said, "Father, I thank you that you have heard me. I knew that you always hear me, but I said this on account of the people standing around, that they may believe that you sent me." When he had said these things, he cried out with a loud voice, "Lazarus, come out." The man who had died came out, his hands and feet bound with linen strips, and his face wrapped with a cloth. Jesus said to them, "Unbind him, and let him go."

Jesus (in John 11:38-44)

When I was eight years old, my brother and I were living with our mom in the Chicagoland suburbs. Our parents had divorced when I was four and he was one. Making an already typically unfortunate American family situation worse was the fact that my mom really couldn't manage us very well. The divorce hit her hard; she never really recovered. She was broken. She simply couldn't handle two young boys.

Our father lived in another part of the Chicago suburbs, as did both sets of grandparents. His parents' home was my favorite place in the world.

Grandma and grandpa were there, of course and that was enough to make the place pretty much perfect. Grandpa had built a tall, sturdy swing in the back yard. We had all the crayons in the world to color with (or, in the case of one interesting cousin, eat). There were Tinker Toys and Legos. There was a chalk board and even a little piano. It was paradise.

By the time I was eight and my little brother was five, we were pretty much running wild. Fortunately, back in the late '70s, when this was going on, kids "running wild" had a very different meaning than it does now. But the bottom line was that we were terribly undisciplined and well on our way to becoming the typical sort of adult disasters that routinely result from broken home situations where overwhelmed mothers are abandoned to fend for themselves.

It was in this context that my father took it upon himself to start doing something uncharacteristically considerate and helpful by picking us up for school each morning. Even at eight, I was already a routine school-skipper, so this newfound fatherly involvement came at a very good time.

One morning in December, dad came by our apartment, we got in his car, and he asked, "You wanna go to Grandma and Grandpa's?"

Instead of to school, you mean? Was this a trick question? Or just a stupid one?

"Yes!" two beaming boys howled after a moment of stunned, cautious silence.

Little did we know when we answered that Grandma and Grandpa had, just that week, moved from their home a few miles from ours to a far away, exotic land called "Arkansas".

We were being kidnapped.

Roughly nine hours later, two boys who'd known nothing but Chicagoland living were taken deeper and deeper into a mystical, wonderful, wooded land known as "The Ozarks". We went through Missouri and on into this "Arkansas" place that had been mentioned to us for the first time just earlier that day.

Waiting nervously in Arkansas for the safe arrival of their son and two grandchildren were Ruth and Daniel, also known as: Grandma and Grandpa.

The sun had gone down and Grandpa was waiting outside in his pickup, radio on and coffee on deck. When we finally rolled into the driveway, he was out of the truck like a shot, and ran around to meet me before I could even finish opening the door to get out. When I did get out, he leaned down, beaming with a broad smile on his face, put one hand on each of my shoulders and looked me straight in the eyes.

"You're a Razorback now."

I had no idea what that meant, but it sounded very cool.

SUPERNATURAL FOOLISHNESS

*For **the word of the cross is folly to those who are perishing**, but to us who are being saved it is the power of God. For it is written,*
"I will destroy the wisdom of the wise,
and the discernment of the discerning I will thwart."
*Where is the one who is wise? Where is the scribe? Where is the debater of this age? Has not God made foolish the wisdom of the world? For **since, in the wisdom of God, the world did not know God through wisdom, it pleased God through the folly of what we preach to save those who believe**.*

1 Corinthians 1:18-21 (Bold emphasis added)

And we know that for those who love God all things work together for good, for those who are called according to his purpose. For those whom he foreknew he also predestined to be conformed to the image of his Son, in order that he might be the firstborn among many brothers. And those whom he predestined he also called, and those whom he called he also justified, and those whom he justified he also glorified.

Romans 8:28-30

There are so many reasons to love, exalt, and proclaim the supernatural Gospel of Jesus Christ, chief among them so that we might glorify God through obedience. And it is though this obedience that every truly good thing that we would ever hope, dream and pray for becomes possible.

As we finally begin to fully embrace His command to bring a supernatural weapon to the war against the flesh so that the dead might be saved and His Kingdom might be advanced right here and right now, we will benefit greatly through the prayerful consideration of a few important questions:

1. Do we believe that those who are lost in rebellion are living, breathing, walking, and often laughing from the very edge of an eternity defined exclusively by God's righteous, holy wrath and judgment?

2. Do we believe that, in the whole, true Gospel of Jesus Christ, we have been given the one and only supernaturally empowered weapon capable of saving these people from that unfathomably bleak fate?

3. Will we use this weapon, no matter the cost to us in the process?

As our mission for His purpose depends so much on our answers to these questions, let's take a moment to consider each of them in some detail.

The Proper (and Inevitable) Fate of Every Rebel

> *I charge you in the presence of God and of Christ Jesus, who is to judge the living and the dead, and by his appearing and his kingdom: preach the word; be ready in season and out of season; reprove, rebuke, and exhort, with complete patience and teaching.*
>
> 2 Timothy 4:1-2

> *For I am not ashamed of the gospel, for it is the power of God for salvation to everyone who believes...*
>
> Romans 1:16

Do we believe that those who are lost in rebellion are living, breathing, walking, and often laughing from the very edge of an eternity defined exclusively by God's righteous, holy wrath and judgment? To understand this truth as we walk, talk, play, and interact with the lost on a day to day basis is an early essential step towards cultivating the sort of passion for the salvation of the lost that will make our proclamation of the hard truths of the Gospel not only easier, but a true joy.

Consider the woman with the coffee cup in her hand, freely sharing her utter disinterest in the things of God, and, in doing so, announcing to all with ears to hear that she is as lost as can be. She seems content. She seems happy. She seems accomplished. And by the standards of a dark and dying world, she may well be all of those things.

But she is damned. And unless something happens – something supernatural – that damnation will be eternal in duration.

Now think of your friends or family members who are in a similar situation. See their faces in your mind. Hear their voices. And understand that they stand, in this moment, with this passing heartbeat, a razor's edge from an eternity of exclusive exposure to the unmitigated wrath of a holy God.

These are people. People that we claim to love. People that we are commanded to love.

Consider them as, in light of biblical truth, they will be 10, 100, and 1,000 years from now. And make no mistake: the question is not whether they will "be", but where.

That should keep us up at night. That is our concern. Doing all that we can to bring them from the kingdom of death and into His Kingdom of life is our mission; the mission that He has given us, and as is the case with all missions He ordains, He has provided us with the necessary tool for its otherwise impossible completion.

In this instance, that tool is the perfect, unstoppable, irresistible, supernatural whole Gospel of Jesus Christ.

OUR SUPERNATURAL SWORD

Let us therefore strive to enter that rest, so that no one may fall by the same sort of disobedience. For the word of God is living and active, sharper than any two-edged sword, piercing to the division of soul and of spirit, of joints and of marrow, and discerning the thoughts and intentions of the heart.

Hebrews 4:11-12

In all circumstances take up the shield of faith, with which you can extinguish all the flaming darts of the evil one; and take the helmet of salvation, and the sword of the Spirit, which is the word of God

Ephesians 6:16-17

Do we believe that, in the whole, true Gospel of Jesus Christ, we have been given the one and only supernaturally empowered weapon capable of saving these people from that unfathomably bleak fate? If we believe this, as we must, then we are without excuse. We must use it.

Challenges to this perspective come early, often, and from every possible angle out there on the cultural battlefield. The enemy, when he cannot entirely prevent us from engaging him, will do everything within his ability to prevent us from making full use of our perfect weapon. Most often, this dulling of its supernatural edge will come through the removal of the hard things – the hard truths – associated with the whole Gospel of Christ.

God is holy? Well, okay, most folks can go along with that, but just see how well the whole "man is born evil" thing goes over with the garden variety zombie. Tell 'em that all men are born hating God and see how they howl. Things can get ugly fast, and while sometimes this will be because we've not been kind enough or gracious enough or patient enough, but sometimes it will simply be because it is precisely the sort of hard truth that sin-lovers, flesh obsessed rebels hate. And when they hear this hated message, they will hate the messenger…until and unless they are supernaturally saved by the very God who has commanded His people to bring this hated message – this "foolishness" - to those who hate Him and "are perishing". It is this tool that He has ordained for conversion and it is this tool that we must take to battle…in its entirety.

When we seek to remove the necessary edge of this supernatural Sword of Truth, it's as though we are waving a sheathed weapon in the air, making fools of ourselves and a mockery of our King, all while bringing a smile to a suddenly more-comfortable-than-ever enemy.

If we want to win, we have to take this Sword out of its sheath and bring its edge to the very neck of every lie of the enemy.

In doing so – and *only* in doing so – will we save the lost we claim to love.

If we refuse to use this weapon, all is lost. Our lost friends are doomed. Our lost family members are doomed. All on our watch…

But if we embrace our King's command and take hold of the supernatural weapon He has prepared for this sacred mission, no angel, demon, man, or zombie can keep us from the victories that He has promised.

THE PRICE OF VICTORY

For God so loved the world, that he gave his only Son, that whoever believes in him should not perish but have eternal life. For God did not send his Son into the world to condemn the world, but in order that the world might be saved through him. Whoever believes in him is not condemned, but whoever does not believe is condemned already, because he has not believed in the name of the only Son of God. And this is the judgment: the light has come into the world, and people loved the darkness rather than the light because their works were evil.

John 3:16-19

*And **you will be hated** by all for my name's sake. But the one who endures to the end will be saved.*

Mark 13:13 (Bold emphasis added)

Will we use this weapon – the supernatural whole Gospel of Jesus Christ – no matter the cost? In this question, we have the opportunity to explore the many opportunities that we will have to suffer persecution for the sake of Christ, His Word, and His Kingdom.

Yes, I said "opportunities to suffer". And I meant it.

Consider the following passages from the Gospel of Matthew:

> "Behold, I am sending you out as sheep in the midst of wolves, so be wise as serpents and innocent as doves. Beware of men, for they will deliver you over to courts

and flog you in their synagogues, and you will be dragged before governors and kings for my sake, to bear witness before them and the Gentiles. When they deliver you over, do not be anxious how you are to speak or what you are to say, for what you are to say will be given to you in that hour. For it is not you who speak, but the Spirit of your Father speaking through you. Brother will deliver brother over to death, and the father his child, and children will rise against parents and have them put to death, and you will be hated by all for my name's sake. But the one who endures to the end will be saved. When they persecute you in one town, flee to the next, for truly, I say to you, you will not have gone through all the towns of Israel before the Son of Man comes.

"A disciple is not above his teacher, nor a servant above his master. It is enough for the disciple to be like his teacher, and the servant like his master. If they have called the master of the house Beelzebul, how much more will they malign those of his household.

"So have no fear of them, for nothing is covered that will not be revealed, or hidden that will not be known. What I tell you in the dark, say in the light, and what you hear whispered, proclaim on the housetops. And do not fear those who kill the body but cannot kill the soul. Rather fear him who can destroy both soul and body in hell." (Matthew 10:16-28)

"Do not think that I have come to bring peace to the earth. I have not come to bring peace, but a sword. For I have come to set a man against his father, and a daughter against her mother, and a daughter-in-law against her mother-in-law. And a person's enemies will be those of his own household. Whoever loves father or mother more than me is not worthy of me, and whoever loves son or daughter more than me is not worthy of me. And whoever does not take his cross and follow me is not worthy of me. Whoever finds his life will lose it, and whoever loses his life for my sake will find it." (Matthew 10:34-39)

So much of what Jesus says so clearly here is so at odds with the strategies, concerns, and general practices of not only the culture at large, but American Churchianity in particular, that it's hard to even imagine what might happen if half of the professing evangelicals in the nation actually accepted, embraced, and ran with the concepts contained therein.

If that were to happen, the world would be changed without a doubt…and that is precisely the point.

We have that power.

We have that mission.

And we have the perfect weapon…it's in our hands…

…and if we use it, as commanded, we will be hated. Not "might" or "may be", but will be hated. And we get a good sense as to why when we consider the following passage from the book of Romans:

> What shall we say then? Is there injustice on God's part? By no means! For he says to Moses, "I will have mercy on whom I have mercy, and I will have compassion on whom I have compassion." So then it depends not on human will or exertion, but on God, who has mercy. For the Scripture says to Pharaoh, "For this very purpose I have raised you up, that I might show my power in you, and that my name might be proclaimed in all the earth." So then he has mercy on whomever he wills, and he hardens whomever he wills.
>
> You will say to me then, "Why does he still find fault? For who can resist his will?" But who are you, O man, to

answer back to God? Will what is molded say to its molder, "Why have you made me like this?" Has the potter no right over the clay, to make out of the same lump one vessel for honorable use and another for dishonorable use? What if God, desiring to show his wrath and to make known his power, has endured with much patience vessels of wrath prepared for destruction, in order to make known the riches of his glory for vessels of mercy, which he has prepared beforehand for glory— even us whom he has called, not from the Jews only but also from the Gentiles (Romans 9:14-24)

In this passage, we find the very essence of unpopularity. A Gospel defined by concepts such as these is what the world tends to label "unmarketable", and that is a great sin in this purpose-driven age.

It is the obsession with marketability - or zombie appeal – that has produced, over the last century or so, the modern "gospel message" of American Churchianity. This has been the path to first a dulled sword, then a sheathed sword, and finally a shelved sword, leaving only world-friendly, man-appeasing, flesh-feeding words left as the primary message with which an apostate church connects with the world it adores.

We are called – you and I – to do everything that we can, right here and now, to reverse this course; to drop the worldly approaches, pick up the Sword of Truth, sharpen it, master it, and bring it to battle with the full intention of using it to cut the enemy to and through the bone at each and every opportunity that we have – and there will be many.

It is time to unsheathe and use this weapon. Our King is soon to return in judgment, and when He does, all of the zombies will be swept away. They will be forever damned; eternally cemented into the wrath-filled position that they teeter before so obliviously at this very moment.

In the meantime, we have a fleeting opportunity; the opportunity to preach salvation to those who are lost – dead in rebellion – and, in doing so, bring them from death into life and into His Kingdom…not by our reasonable or pragmatic means, but by His supernatural "foolishness", which is the pure, undiluted Gospel of Jesus Christ.

With that weapon in use, we will liberate the dead, adding scores to His service while marching from victory to victory, grinding the rubble of crushed enemy strongholds under our heels as we go.

9

RAZING HELL

TAKING THE TRUTH WAR TO ZOMBIELAND

TAKING THE TRUTH WAR TO ZOMBIELAND

For though we walk in the flesh, we are not waging war according to the flesh. For the weapons of our warfare are not of the flesh but have divine power to destroy strongholds. We destroy arguments and every lofty opinion raised against the knowledge of God, and take every thought captive to obey Christ

2 Corinthians 10:3-5

"Christians are not left in the world by accident but are placed there on divine assignment from their Lord."

John MacArthur

For mostly obvious reasons, I'd never been to a "gay pride" parade before, even though, heading into the summer of 2010, I'd lived in cities like Seattle before where such events have long been a part of the established cultural norm. Yet when June, 2010 rolled around, and I was again living in Seattle, just a stone's throw from the Space Needle, I decided it was time to take a closer look at what progressive culture had to offer.

While I would surely have been completely content to ride out and avoid another fine installment of progressivism on parade under normal circumstances, I had recently become involved with a ministry seeking to address the issue of homosexuality from a biblical perspective. With this subject more on my mind as a result, and the big gay event about to unfortunately unfold mere yards from my couch, I decided to take advantage of this unique opportunity to do a little recon.

So off I went, walking through the beautiful summer Seattle day en route to the epicenter of the looming celebration of rebellion, also known as 4th & Pine. There I camped out, settling into a good spot to grab some pictures as the parade participants began their journey down Fourth Ave and, after a few turns, basically to my apartment's front door. (Ouch!)

As I was taking in the pre-game atmosphere, I was struck by the contrast in the gathering crowd. While the gathered mass of humanity certainly sported a significant contingent of the sort of flamboyantly fabulous sorts you might imagine (and then wish you hadn't), the striking thing to me was just how plain Jane, white bread suburban the majority of the crowd really was. The coming parade and all that it symbolized clearly had the support of the mainstream here in Seattle, however odd that mainstream might be when compared to the rest of the nation.

The weight of this reality hit me a few moments later as I settled into my spot, set my camera, and noticed three little girls sitting in front of the crowd on the edge of the parade path across the street just in front of the downtown Seattle Macy's store (a proud sponsor of the event). The three of them looked to be somewhere between the ages of six and nine, all well groomed and dressed, as though they'd been prepped for the first day of school. There they sat, sweet and innocent, looking on and awaiting the show, as though it was the Fourth of July and we were on Main Street in Mayberry awaiting some good, wholesome, all-American fun.

THE PARADE OF PAGANISM IN POST-CHRISTIAN AMERICA

> "No sin that a person commits has more built-in pitfalls, problems and destructiveness than sexual sin. It has broken more marriages, shattered more homes, caused more heartache and disease, and destroyed more lives than alcohol and drugs combined. It causes lying, stealing, cheating and killing, as well as bitterness, hatred, slander, gossip and unforgiveness."
>
> John MacArthur

So it was that on an otherwise beautiful, sunny Seattle day, surrounded by every good thing and every "good" seeming sort of person, from smiling children to soccer moms, I felt as though I was witnessing a well-orchestrated, large-scale, multi-layered demonstration of the truth of the Lord as revealed in His perfect Word. The parade seemed to be less determined to follow a 4th Ave Seattle route than it was destined to follow the road to Romans, just as God had said it would:

> For the wrath of God is revealed from heaven against all ungodliness and unrighteousness of men, who by their unrighteousness suppress the truth. For what can be known about God is plain to them, because God has shown it to them. For his invisible attributes, namely, his eternal power and divine nature, have been clearly perceived, ever since the creation of the world, in the things that have been made. So they are without excuse.

> For although they knew God, they did not honor him as God or give thanks to him, but they became futile in their thinking, and their foolish hearts were darkened. Claiming to be wise, they became fools, and exchanged the glory of the immortal God for images resembling mortal man and birds and animals and creeping things.
>
> Therefore God gave them up in the lusts of their hearts to impurity, to the dishonoring of their bodies among themselves, because they exchanged the truth about God for a lie and worshiped and served the creature rather than the Creator, who is blessed forever! Amen.
>
> For this reason God gave them up to dishonorable passions. For their women exchanged natural relations for those that are contrary to nature; and the men likewise gave up natural relations with women and were consumed with passion for one another, men committing shameless acts with men and receiving in themselves the due penalty for their error.
>
> And since they did not see fit to acknowledge God, God gave them up to a debased mind to do what ought not to be done. They were filled with all manner of unrighteousness, evil, covetousness, malice. They are full of envy, murder, strife, deceit, maliciousness. They are gossips, slanderers, haters of God, insolent, haughty, boastful, inventors of evil, disobedient to parents, foolish, faithless, heartless, ruthless. Though they know God's decree that those who practice such things deserve to die, they not only do them but give approval to those who practice them. (Romans 1:18-32)

As the celebration officially began and the first floats started their crawl through the cheering masses, even I was unprepared for what was to come. I will not describe much of what I saw here, other than to say that, as I wandered along the parade route snapping pictures of different abominations from different angles, my mind kept returning to those three little girls who were witnessing, from a front row seat, each unfolding, successive display of depravity.

The event was all about pride on many levels, as parades tend to be. It was like watching a triumphant army marching through a conquered city, celebrating the capture of a culture long warred over and finally won.

And of course there were the progressive religionists, leading the procession with their loud, proud claim that "God is love!" and "Jesus loves us as we are!"

So it was that American Churchianity was every bit as much on parade as the cross-dressing, sadomasochism adoring zombies marching along 4th Ave and on towards the Romans Road.

They had religion. Much of it. They had God. The God "that is love". And they even had it all wrapped up in Jesus' name.

As any good zombie will tell you, God "isn't mad at anybody"; He only wants to make them happy. He only wants to give them what they want deep down inside. He only wants to help them to live up to the potential contained in their blackened little hearts. God is ultimately the servant of man – the ultimate tool just waiting to be used by those enlightened enough to understand this truth and bold enough to seize the opportunity that it presented for their self-glorification.

As I watched the parade roll on, it wasn't hard to picture the Ark of the Covenant, at least as imagined in *Raiders*, leading the way; inspiring and empowering the procession of a culture conquering and seemingly invincible army as they happily celebrated their liberation of America from Christianity.

And Indiana Jones was nowhere to be found.

Where are true heroes when you really need em?

(Hint: They're precisely where He wants them to be.)

Conquering Zombieland

"It would be easy to show that at our present rate of progress the kingdoms of this world never could become the kingdom of our Lord and of His Christ. Indeed, many in the Church are giving up the idea of it except on the occasion of the advent of Christ, which, as it chimes in with our own idleness, is likely to be a popular doctrine. I myself believe that King Jesus will reign, and the idols be utterly abolished; but I expect the same power which turned the world upside down once will still continue to do it. The Holy Ghost would never suffer the imputation to rest upon His holy name that He was not able to convert the world."

Charles Haddon Spurgeon

For consider your calling, brothers: not many of you were wise according to worldly standards, not many were powerful, not many were of noble birth. But God chose what is foolish in the world to shame the wise; God chose what is weak in the world to shame the strong; God chose what is low and despised in the world, even things that are not, to bring to nothing things that are, so that no human being might boast in the presence of God. And because of him you are in Christ Jesus, who became to us wisdom from God, righteousness and sanctification and redemption, so that, as it is written, "Let the one who boasts, boast in the Lord."

1 Corinthians 1:26-31

Brokenness defines the aftermath of rebellion. In the strictest sense, rebels do not break God's law. Rather, they are broken upon it. And this brokenness was the unintended featured attribute of the 2010 Seattle Gay Pride Parade.

That particular celebration of the dead is but one footnote event in a long line of progressive degeneration made possible in no small part through the near-century-long efforts of American Churchianity – the religion most responsible for the decline of biblical Christianity in the West and the brokenness that has been left in the wake of that transformative shift from light toward darkness.

Zombie "culture" paints a vivid picture of this brokenness, and seems to enjoy doing so more and more with each successive step taken into the darkness. Such is the nature of rebellion.

And every unrepentant rebel – every zombie – is an individual representation of the unique ways in which brokenness and dysfunction can come together to define the life of those who reject truth and its Author.

As we covered at the beginning of this journey through *Apathetic Christianity*, there are several specific areas of influence where the professing church in America has played a vital role in bringing a once overtly Christianity-inclined nation into its current man-centered, putrefied zombie state.

These areas include:

- **Apathetic Leadership**
- **Apathetic Family Life**
- **Apathetic Education**
- **Apathetic Theology and Doctrine**
- **Apathetic Discipline**
- **Apathetic Politics**

An essential early step toward victory on the battlefield is to identify and understand enemy strategies and strongholds. To that end, we will now take a moment to elaborate on these areas of distinction between orthodox biblical Christianity and the apostate American version that has come to define our nation.

TARGET ACQUISITION

> *For though we walk in the flesh, we are not waging war according to the flesh. For the weapons of our warfare are not of the flesh but have divine power to destroy strongholds. We destroy arguments and every lofty opinion raised against the knowledge of God, and take every thought captive to obey Christ*
>
> 2 Corinthians 10:3-5

> "Doctrine matters. What you believe about God, the gospel, the nature of man, and every major truth addressed in Scripture filters down to every area of your life. You and I will never rise above our view of God and our understanding of His Word."
>
> John MacArthur

In order to tear down an enemy stronghold, one must first identify said stronghold. Sounds simple enough, and it is. But as tends to be the case when human beings and simple truths get together, the problem lies not in a lack of knowledge or information – the truth has been made plain to all with eyes to see and ears to hear. The problem lies in our struggle against *obedience*; our resistance to *submission*. And for most of us, it is the inherent appeal of man-centered religion and religious practices that taps into our residual inclination towards disobedience and rebellion.

While we all recognize the folly of the Nazis in *Raiders of the Lost Ark*, who actually believed that they could manipulate the power of God for their own purposes, we often demonstrate a truly fantastic blind spot when it comes to our inherent inclination to do the same. All of human (and-human-centered) religious history demonstrates this. The Jews of Jesus' day used a ridiculously unbiblical system as their substitute for truth and tool by which they would earn God's approval and claim His favor as their own. The Roman Catholic Church did the same in the time of Martin Luther. And American Churchianity is doing this very thing at this very moment.

Now consider again the "gay pride" parade in Seattle. And imagine again the *Raiders*-style Ark in the hands of that mob. Figuratively, if not literally, this mob seeks to use the power of God – and the very name of Jesus – to actively promote an agenda that stands in stark contrast to His clearly expressed will. Yet they pursue this path anyway, precisely because they view the Jesus they've made up in their minds and the religion associated with him as means to an end; merely as tools to attain their personal happiness.

How different is this from the Judaism of Jesus' time on earth? How different is it from the Romanism that dominated prior to the Reformation? And how different is it from the American Churchianity of today?

Do we see exaltation of and submission to the clear pronouncements of Scripture as the foundation of American Churchianity, or do we instead see just another phony system, Ark, or tool used as cover for just the latest incarnation of the man-centered religion to come down the pike? When we go down that list of categories and concerns, do we see the standards of man or the standards of God as the banners under which positions have been formed and "ministries" built?

BIBLICALLY FOCUSED VS BIBLICALLY APATHETIC

"Fearing God has two aspects. The first is reverence. It is a sacred awe of God's utter holiness. It involves the kind of respect and veneration that results in fear in the presence of such absolute majesty. The second aspect is fear of God's displeasure. Genuine faith acknowledges God's right to chasten, His right to punish, and His right to judge."

John MacArthur

All Scripture is breathed out by God and profitable for teaching, for reproof, for correction, and for training in righteousness, *that the man of God may be competent, equipped for **every** good work.*

2 Timothy 3:16-17 (Bold emphasis added)

If a fearful reverence of the Lord is the beginning of all good things, as His perfect Word makes perfectly clear, then we need look no further than an apathetic approach to His nature and revelation in order to properly identify a position, philosophy, or position of the enemy. Target acquisition really can be just that easy.

This doesn't require deep theological dissection. The questions are simple and the answers are not hard to find.

Do we see biblically focused leadership or biblically apathetic leadership at the helm of American Churchianity?

Do we see biblically focused family policies or biblically apathetic family policies embraced by the "church" in America? Do we see the biblical model for family exalted and supported by the American church, or do we find American Churchianity using secular models and philosophies to, among other things, actually displace the family from its central position in favor of the "church"?

Do we see biblically focused education standards or biblically apathetic education standards embraced by the "church" in America? Do we see Christ-centered education proclaimed as essential by American Churchianity, or do we find rampant accommodation of an utterly Christ-less system of public "education"?

Do we see biblically focused doctrine and theology or biblically apathetic philosophy at the core of "church" policy in America? Do we find a love for the Lord and His holy nature demonstrated by a deep desire for and respect of His teachings, or do we find concepts such as "doctrine" and "theology" dismissed as, at best, unnecessary extras reserved for spiritual elites?

Do we see biblically focused standards of discipline or biblically apathetic standards of discipline embraced by the "church" in America? Do we find a love for the Lord demonstrated by a desire for the purity of His bride, or do we find things like biblical church discipline dismissed out of hand as relics of an unmarketable past?

Do we find biblically prescribed, Kingdom politics or biblically apathetic "progressive" politics emanating from the "church" in America? Do we witness a love for the Lord through the desire of His people to submit *all* things – including their political will and action – to His service, or do we instead see a move to sequester certain areas of life – including our business lives, our political lives, and our sexual lives – in order to keep them "free" from His standards?

These are questions that have been asked and largely answered in earlier chapters. But it is important here to note two themes that pervade these issues and help us to easily spot the enemy stronghold that we are commanded by our King to destroy:

1. **Rebellion.** – The theme of rebellion is apparent and is always a dead giveaway where the identity of an enemy stronghold is concerned. In every instance – and always accompanied by a long list of reasons/excuses/explanations – there is an open rejection of clear (and often excruciatingly and redundantly clear) biblical teaching in favor of worldly, seeker-sensitive, "pragmatic" alternatives.

2. **Man is exalted and God is diminished.** – "The fear of the Lord" is set aside in favor of the fear of the opinion of man. Every time. This is another universally reliable indicator of anti-Christian positions and philosophies.

These are the two attributes that always apply to all who would seek the power of God for themselves – those who would seek their own Ark to use for their own purposes. Theirs are the armies that have come to make war on truth and its Author. And these are the armies that we are called to oppose with that very truth on His behalf, by His grace and to His glory. Insofar as we are obedient in this calling, we are guaranteed victory – a victory that is assured not by our might, but by His decree.

In this, we secure success through submission even before the battle plays out in what we call time – no matter the name or nature of the phony Ark trotted out by the armies of our enemies.

Through submission to His will, the battle is already won…*in every meaningful way.*

This counterintuitive truth, when properly understood, is supernaturally empowering. As such, it is a true super-weapon; the likes of which the zombie religion of American Christianity simply cannot understand, much less defend against.

It is the predestined winning shot in the war against rebellion. It is the death knell of zombie religion in America…and everywhere else.

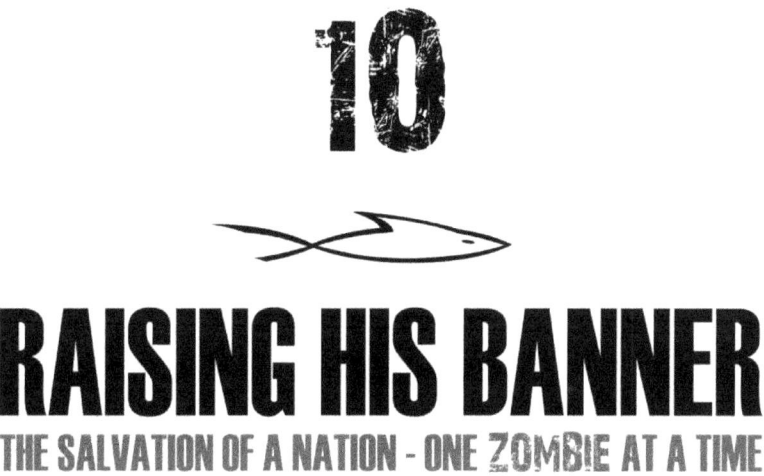

10

RAISING HIS BANNER
THE SALVATION OF A NATION - ONE ZOMBIE AT A TIME

RAISING HIS BANNER
THE SALVATION OF A NATION - ONE ZOMBIE AT A TIME

And if it is evil in your eyes to serve the LORD, choose this day whom you will serve, whether the gods your fathers served in the region beyond the River, or the gods of the Amorites in whose land you dwell. But as for me and my house, we will serve the LORD.

Joshua 25:15

"We are not diplomats but prophets, and our message is not a compromise, but an ultimatum."

A.W. Tozer

Dr. Walter Martin, best known as the original voice of *The Bible Answer Man* radio broadcast, was a well-known Christian apologist and author. When asked how he advised fellow believers to go about the process of preparing to effectively defend the Christian faith, he relayed a story that unfolded between him and a friend of his years earlier.

His friend was an officer with the Secret Service, and one of his primary duties was to train new recruits in the art of detecting counterfeit money. Hearing of this interesting similarity between what this man's job called for – training others to detect faulty bills – and what his own calling was – to train Christians in the detection of falsehood for the purpose of defending truth, Martin asked, "How do you teach this? Do you spend a lot of your time with these new recruits going over the latest and greatest in counterfeiting techniques and counterfeit products?"

The answer was a semi-surprising, "No. Not much at all."

The agent went on to confirm a principle that Dr. Martin had long embraced and advocated where the detection of falsehood was concerned, namely, that the best defense against lies is to know the truth, or, as the agent put it, "We get real cash into the hands of the agents and keep it there. They count it, stack it, feel it, and move it in their fingers and in front of their eyes constantly. They become so familiar with the real deal that when a fake turns up, even if they can't immediately tell why it is a fake, they just know that something is off the mark. They become able to naturally detect counterfeits by virtue of their familiarity with the true original that has been imperfectly copied."

This is the key to advancing the Kingdom and defending it from any would be competitor: *We must first know His truth.*

For us, this is the first act of obedience.

For the zombie religion of American Churchianity

REBELLION – THE MURDER OF TRUTH AND BEAUTY

You said in your heart,
  'I will ascend to heaven;
above the stars of God
  I will set my throne on high;
I will sit on the mount of assembly
  in the far reaches of the north;
  I will ascend above the heights of the clouds;
  I will make myself like the Most High.'

Isaiah 14:13-14

Jesus said to them, "If God were your Father, you would love me, for I came from God and I am here. I came not of my own accord, but he sent me. Why do you not understand what I say? It is because you cannot bear to hear my word. You are of your father the devil, and your will is to do your father's desires. He was a murderer from the beginning, and has nothing to do with the truth, because there is no truth in him. When he lies, he speaks out of his own character, for he is a liar and the father of lies."

John 8:42-44

Everything against which we contend is built upon one concept in action: Rebellion.

Rebellion against the lordship and rule of Christ is the defining, pervasive course of this dark and dying world. It is the essential spirit of all expressed sin. It is born of pride in the self, and its every aim is to justify the self's ascension to the throne of sovereignty. It is the natural and inevitable expression of pride in action.

Rebellion is the anti-Kingdom state of being. Just as the zombie cultures and kingdoms are all image-bearers of truth that have been bent and broken into polar opposites of what God will have in His Kingdom, so too has the life, peace, and joy sustaining power of obedience to Christ been radically perverted into the rebellion-dominated shadowland in which we live.

We are here for great purpose. A miraculous purpose.

We are here to win the war against the apathetic life of zombie culture and religion, not through brilliant arguments, pragmatic accommodations or irresistible marketing plans aimed at "reaching the zombie" or any similar sort of true foolishness. We are called to win this otherwise hopeless and doomed world through the supernatural power of submission to the rightful Ruler and King of both this fading world and the perfect creation to come.

As such, obedience is the banner that we are called to lift up and hold high in *every* circumstance, over *every* battlefield, above *every* realm, in *every* arena, and covering *every* concern, concept, and category under consideration. *Everything* is to be brought under the banner of obedience – obedience not to a system, a theology, an order, or a concept, but to a King. *Our* King. The one true and soon returning King Jesus.

This is our mission.

Herein is our power to win the otherwise unwinnable and save the otherwise unsalvageable. We really can do what this world is so desperate to have us believe is impossible.

As with all else that is of the world, this "assurance of defeat" is a lie.

Ultimately, it is nothing more powerful or less pathetic than the dying gasp of failing rebellion.

THE SUPERNATURAL MIRACLE OF OBEDIENCE

"Righteous wrath is no less noble than love, since both coexist in God."

John MacArthur

...the people spoke against God and against Moses, "Why have you brought us up out of Egypt to die in the wilderness? For there is no food and no water, and we loathe this worthless food." Then the LORD sent fiery serpents among the people, and they bit the people, so that many people of Israel died. And the people came to Moses and said, "We have sinned, for we have spoken against the LORD and against you. Pray to the LORD, that he take away the serpents from us." So Moses prayed for the people. And the LORD said to Moses, "Make a fiery serpent and set it on a pole, and everyone who is bitten, when he sees it, shall live." So Moses made a bronze serpent and set it on a pole. And if a serpent bit anyone, he would look at the bronze serpent and live.

Numbers 21:5-9

The wrath of God will rightly fall upon the rebellious and the apathetic. This judgment is coming, and soon.

As the perfect world to come will be fueled and defined by undiluted passion for truth and beauty, apathy can have no role there – not so much as the slightest shadow in which to hide. It will be gone. Completely gone.

Apathetic family life, apathetic worship, apathetic prayer, apathetic economics, apathetic theology, apathetic education, and apathetic politics...all gone...forever. As they all fit hand in glove with sin and lead to pain, destruction, and death wherever they take root, these apathetic pursuits must and will be banished, and they will be banished here and now as we, in obedience to our King, deploy the supernatural banner of obedience.

Every area and realm in this creation can and will be conquered by His name and for His Kingdom, if only we will *obey*.

It is vital that we ignore the zombie propaganda and embrace the notion that every enemy held, zombie infested realm is nothing more intimidating or less inviting that territory waiting – *begging* even – to be claimed for Him, by His grace, to His glory...through *our* obedience.

He has ordained this to be so. He has called us to an action – obedience in a world of rebellion – and promised ultimate victory.

With this perspective in mind, we must expect that every realm is awaiting the conquering armies of the Kingdom, and those armies will march when – and only when – we obey.

This obedience will come in every area and in every moment of life. As we obey, the Kingdom will advance. As we rebel, it will retreat. It really is that simple. So simple a zombie can understand it, you might say...which is precisely why they so desperately feed us mountains of death-enabling defeatist propaganda at every turn.

The dead will do *anything* to justify and preserve their apathy toward Christ's lordship.

PASSION'S TRIUMPH IS APATHY'S END

Just as it was in the days of Noah, so will it be in the days of the Son of Man. They were eating and drinking and marrying and being given in marriage, until the day when Noah entered the ark, and the flood came and destroyed them all. Likewise, just as it was in the days of Lot — they were eating and drinking, buying and selling, planting and building, but on the day when Lot went out from Sodom, fire and sulfur rained from heaven and destroyed them all — so will it be on the day when the Son of Man is revealed.

Luke 17:26-30

"The results of ignoring church discipline are catastrophic. Gross public sin is overlooked, ignored, and tolerated. The fellowship of believers deteriorates to the point where it's indistinguishable from the unbelieving world. God's people forfeit the credibility of their testimony. And self-deceived sinners happily remain in the local church, unaware of their need for true repentance and faith."

John MacArthur

As we dive deeper and deeper into the perfect Word of God, we will come to know our Lord more intimately, so that we might better love what He loves and hate what He hates. Through obedience to His command to live in and through His Word, we will find every good thing for which we long. We will find the growth, depth, peace, love, and joy that are otherwise unattainable – *only* through this obedience.

As we submit to His call to personal communion with Him in "prayer without ceasing", we will find the reality of relationship at a level that is otherwise impossible. We will desire to know His truth, we will celebrate the opportunity to learn His theology, and we will relish every newly uncovered reality of His identity as we obey His command to study and pray.

As we seek to court, marry, and begin families on biblical foundations, and then nurture them by the same standards – raising *our* children and educating *our* children *personally* and with an explicit emphasis on the lordship of Christ in *all* things – we will inherently banish the apathetic family life that now permeates our culture and promotes its ongoing rot. We will reclaim the essential realm of family – replacing the apathetic counterfeit with the vibrant, beautiful and true version – *only* through this obedience.

As we obey His loving command to connect with and embrace our fellow Common Believers – brothers and sisters and joint heirs of the Kingdom – we will find matchless peace while inherently banishing the countless apathetic attributes of any community not overtly centered on Him. In this, we will reclaim the realms of community and culture – one transformed gathering at a time, and *only* through this submission.

As we obey His command to love Him with all of our mind, body, spirit, and *vote*, we will bring the political realm into proper subjugation, and in the wake of such a transformation…can you even imagine it? So fervent and frenzied have been the cries of the dead against this possibility that even this concept even in the context of this book and even in the clear light of perfect Scripture is likely difficult for many Common Believer's to accept, at least initially. But make no mistake: This is truth. The political realm is ours for the taking because it is His to deliver.

We are not here to win, per se.

But we are here to fight.

We fight out of obedience to His command to do so and then we leave the victory – and all glory that comes with it – to Him.

He will deliver.

If only we will obey.

THE SUPERNATURAL POWER OF SUBMISSION

> "..as Moses lifted up the serpent in the wilderness, so must the Son of Man be lifted up, that whoever believes in him may have eternal life. For God so loved the world, that he gave his only Son, that whoever believes in him should not perish but have eternal life."
>
> John 3:14-16

> "…when John called Jesus "the Lamb of God," neither he nor his hearers had in mind anything remotely similar to what the average, modern, man-on-the-street might think of if he heard someone called a "lamb." John did not mean Jesus was sweet, cuddly, nice, or cute. In fact, John wasn't referring to Jesus' personality at all. He meant that Jesus was the sinless Sacrifice for the world."
>
> David Chilton, *Paradise Restored*

The Kingdom is built on and for passion, truth and beauty, and it is built in such a manner and for such a purpose because it is to be a clear, pure reflection of the nature of its Creator.

The ultimate establishment of this Kingdom is the ultimate end of apathy…in every realm.

In this, the identity of Christ finds its rightful place as the centerpiece of all that is worthy of contemplation.

The response to Christ the King's clear commands – the choice of submission or rebellion – when made by an individual, a family, a town, a city, a nation or a culture, will always and completely define their life. Where rebellion persists, its willful victim is consigned to the apathetic life. Where obedience and submission to Christ are embraced, liberation from apathy and entry into a world defined by truth, passion, and beauty is always the supernaturally wondrous result.

The Bride, a reflection of purity through her obedience and adoration of Christ, her Groom, will rule and reign with Him for the eternal future to come. His chosen people will know perfect adventure, exploration, expression, and relationship in the context of a perfect, ever-expanding cosmos awaiting their discovery and subjugation. All of this will begin and continue without end through loving obedience to the perfect Master.

The Whore, the essence of self-centered rebellion, will be swept away. All who embrace her narcissistic, self-referential, self-obsessed spirit of anti-Christ will suffer His perfect, holy wrath for eternity as well – all as a right and proper demonstration of his perfectly good and holy attributes of wrath, anger, jealousy, and justice.

These are the fates that await the children of obedience and the children of rebellion.

TRUST, OBEY, AND WIN

Have this mind among yourselves, which is yours in Christ Jesus, who, though he was in the form of God, did not count equality with God a thing to be grasped, but made himself nothing, taking the form of a servant, being born in the likeness of men. And being found in human form, he humbled himself by becoming obedient to the point of death, even death on a cross.

Philippians 2:5-8

"Everyone recognizes that Stephen was Spirit-filled when he was performing wonders. Yet, he was just as Spirit-filled when he was being stoned to death."

Leonard Ravenhill

How do we reach the lady with the coffee who is comfortably going to Hell thanks to the assurances of the zombie religion of American Churchianity?

How do we combat the culture conquering armies marching through the cities of a once Christianity embracing nation with their phony Ark on parade before them and the phony gospel of American Churchianity enabling them?

How do we bring peace, passion, and power to lives now defined by doubt, apathy, and weakness?

We do these and all other worthy things through obedience. Simple, supernatural obedience.

Therein lies the death of death, the establishment of the Kingdom, and the end of all things apathetic…zombies included.

AFTERGLOW

FOR THE LOVE OF THE
KING

THE DEFINING MISSION OF THE COMMON BELIEVER

FOR THE LOVE OF THE KING
THE DEFINING MISSION OF THE COMMON BELIEVER

Hear, O Israel: The LORD our God, the LORD is one. You shall love the LORD your God with all your heart and with all your soul and with all your might.

Deuteronomy 6:4-5

"You shall love the Lord your God with all your heart and with all your soul and with all your mind. This is the great and first commandment."

Jesus (in Matthew 22:37-38)

"If you love me, you will keep my commandments."

Jesus (in John 14:15)

If we truly and completely believe that God is holy, man is evil, the King of kings will soon return to judge His creation by His standards, and that the Gospel command to repent, believe, and be saved from this coming judgment not only secures escape from the righteous wrath of a holy God for those who are supernaturally brought to repentance and belief through its power, but that those who are saved also become adopted sons of the Father and heirs to His perfect Kingdom, then we are inherently immune to apathy. If we really believe that those who are supernaturally saved will rule and reign and grow and explore and create and love and laugh perfectly and eternally, we cannot possibly be apathetic about our Lord or His Gospel. If we believe these things, then apathy is a dead concept for us. It has no place left as it is simply impossible for it to coexist with the vibrant, passionate, powerful life that defines the true Christian walk in practice.

It is the all-consuming fire within us – the Spirit of the living God – that leaves no room for such a thing as apathy. While this might sound obvious and agreeable enough on its face, what we seem to have on our hands in this particular period of American religious history is something of an apathetic take on apathy. So long as this persists, we will continue to suffer from and enable the apathetic worship, apathetic family life, apathetic theology, and apathetic living in general that is described in this book. Until we embrace the call of Christ to make war on sin, and understand that sin is always founded in apathy, be it an apathy regarding the nature of God or His truth, we will witness the continuing decline of what many still like to interestingly refer to as our "Christian nation."

To love the Lord as He is to be loved leaves no room for apathy. Moreover, it leaves no room for the *tolerance* of apathy, and the supernatural power of the Gospel itself confirms this every time it is accurately presented in its pure, undiluted form. When this sort of biblical presentation is made, the truth proclaimed is either adored or despised; there is no genuine apathy to be found. The Gospel annihilates apathy, and we must seek to follow its divine example.

We must make war on it and every one of its apathetic strongholds. Yet even in that "we must make war" statement, the declaration can be misleading…particularly to our often apathetic minds.

We make this war not because we have to, but because we want to…and *desperately* so!

As "new creatures" – supernaturally reborn Common Believers in Christ – we have an innate appetite and love for truth, and this love inspires not only a fervor for its defense, but an obedience to its Author, who has commanded us to take His supernatural Word to the corners of the world.

He has raised us from death to life while we yet hated Him, He has promised that we will rule and reign His creation with Him for the perfect eternity to come, and He has done these things by His grace and for His pleasure. It was *His* pleasure to do this for *us*!
That reality alone should obliterate all apathy from the Christian mind. And, by the grace of God, in time through the perfect work of sanctification, it will.

When we see that an essential part of His Kingdom's advancement is the banishment of all things apathetic, we are one step closer to ultimate victory…an ultimate victory already promised and secured by Him…an ultimate victory that already has us "seated in the heavenly places".

This truth should inspire as nothing else can. It should inspire us to embrace His light as never before and bring it to His world just as He has commanded…all out of love and adoration for the King. If we love Him, we *will* keep this commandment.

COUNTER-REVOLUTIONARY SUBMISSION

"True faith is never seen as passive - it is always obedient."

John MacArthur

"It would have been much easier on the early Christians, of course, if they had preached the popular retreatist doctrine that Jesus is Lord of the "heart", that He is concerned with "spiritual" (meaning non-earthly) conquests, but isn't the least bit interested in political questions; that He is content to be "Lord" in the realm of the spirit, while Caesar is Lord everywhere else (i.e., where we feel it really matters). Such a doctrine would have been no threat whatsoever to the gods of Rome. In fact, Caesar couldn't ask for a more cooperative religion! Toothless, impotent Christianity is a gold mine for statism: It keeps men's attention focused on the clouds while the State picks their pockets and steals their children."

David Chilton, *Days of Vengance*

All of post-Fall human history is defined by rebellion, and rebellion is the antithesis of submission, so it is not surprising that the following three things are true:

1. All mankind is born hating submission.
2. Only those who are supernaturally transformed into "new creatures" in Christ are truly able to even begin to resist

and conquer this inclination toward rebellion, bringing themselves into submission to Him, not out of dry duty, but out of genuine love and adoration.

3. One supernatural consequence of the ultimate advance of the Kingdom of Christ is the elimination of all forms of rebellion, which are all rooted in apathy.

So we see that the evisceration of the apathetic life in all of its forms and practices is a central theme to the advance of His Kingdom, as apathy is an inherent casualty of the elimination of rebellion. As we see this Kingdom advance – one individual at a time, one family at a time, and one community at a time – we will see passion and beauty thrive as never before. And when the vibrant life of true passion that comes through Christ begins to take root and produce more and more fruit, we will be amazed and inspired as never before.

We are already beginning to see this move of God through His people in what seems to many to be an "impossibly dire" situation. We are told that all is really lost already and that, at best, we should just try to hang on 'til Jesus comes to fix it all. Whatever the case, we should resign ourselves to gradual decline and defeat until He divinely intervenes to save the day, or so the apathetically world appeasing line of thought goes.

This ridiculous and explicitly counter-Christian notion is the first hurdle that must be cleared for many who have been successfully confused by zombie religion in America where the role and responsibility of the Common Believer in the advancement of the Kingdom right here and right now is concerned. This is the apathetic barrier that must be crushed so that Kingdom-driven progress can really *begin*, much less find its completion.

Apathetic worship must be actively, enthusiastically, and *lovingly* replaced with the God-exalting, Gospel-proclaiming, sin-indicting, Christ-adoring message that He has ordained for His worship. As we worship and nurture worship properly, we will naturally find ourselves uprooting the secular/pop-culture-driven approaches to family and family life in favor of the biblical models that are essential for His people to thrive and for His Kingdom to be advanced. And what better place to begin than with the concept of instilling the adoration of righteous submission – a concept utterly loathed by the world – than in the God-ordained family. Pastor John MacArthur expressed the essential nature of submission and obedience in the God-ordained family model this way:

> "The message for children is short and simple: obedience - in both attitude and action - is 'right'. It is 'well pleasing to the Lord'. It is honoring to the parents. And it is good for the children - protecting them from a world of evil, prolonging their lives, and bringing them an abundance of blessing."

The more we extricate beautiful concepts such as biblical submission and obedience out from under the mountains of toxic baggage that the world has heaped upon them, the more we will see the sorts of positive changes in our lives, families, and culture that may, at this moment seem impossible.

Through our true and loving submission to Him, all good and great things become not only possible, but promised.

And through our loving submission to Him in His command to proclaim His Gospel to the world, we can see to it that others who are lost to apathy, rebellion, and death might also be supernaturally saved, by His grace and for His glory.

AFTERGLOW

THE RETURNING KING

Then I saw heaven opened, and behold, a white horse! The one sitting on it is called Faithful and True, and in righteousness he judges and makes war. His eyes are like a flame of fire, and on his head are many diadems, and he has a name written that no one knows but himself. He is clothed in a robe dipped in blood, and the name by which he is called is The Word of God. And the armies of heaven, arrayed in fine linen, white and pure, were following him on white horses. From his mouth comes a sharp sword with which to strike down the nations, and he will rule them with a rod of iron. He will tread the winepress of the fury of the wrath of God the Almighty. On his robe and on his thigh he has a name written, King of kings and Lord of lords. (Revelation 19:11-16)

Consider this passage from the book of Revelation and ask yourself, "How can such a vision – a true and accurate representation – of the certain future of this earth and this humanity possibly allow for the accommodation of any apathetic worship, evangelism, family life, or theology?"

The King *is* coming.

He's coming to *judge*.

We have been given and commanded to use the one and only supernatural tool with the power to save those who are lost and currently standing under the righteous condemnation of a just and holy God.

Do we believe this? Just a little, maybe? Or technically? Or not at all?

Anything but a yes followed by action is apathetic.
Read on:

> Then I saw a great white throne and him who was seated on it. From his presence earth and sky fled away, and no place was found for them. And I saw the dead, great and small, standing before the throne, and books were opened. Then another book was opened, which is the book of life. And the dead were judged by what was written in the books, according to what they had done. And the sea gave up the dead who were in it, Death and Hades gave up the dead who were in them, and they were judged, each one of them, according to what they had done. Then Death and Hades were thrown into the lake of fire. This is the second death, the lake of fire. And if anyone's name was not found written in the book of life, he was thrown into the lake of fire. (Revelation 20:11-15)

Again, do we believe this (Rob Bellism notwithstanding)? Do we take it seriously? Does it inform our daily lives?

Or are *we* apathetic?

> Then I saw a new heaven and a new earth, for the first heaven and the first earth had passed away, and the sea was no more. And I saw the holy city, new Jerusalem, coming down out of heaven from God, prepared as a bride adorned for her husband. And I heard a loud voice from the throne saying, "Behold, the dwelling place of God is with man. He will dwell with them, and they will be his people, and God himself will be with them as their God. He will wipe away every tear from their eyes, and death shall be no more, neither shall there be mourning, nor crying, nor pain anymore, for the former things have passed away."

And he who was seated on the throne said, "Behold, I am making all things new." Also he said, "Write this down, for these words are trustworthy and true." And he said to me, "It is done! I am the Alpha and the Omega, the beginning and the end. To the thirsty I will give from the spring of the water of life without payment. The one who conquers will have this heritage, and I will be his God and he will be my son. But as for the cowardly, the faithless, the detestable, as for murderers, the sexually immoral, sorcerers, idolaters, and all liars, their portion will be in the lake that burns with fire and sulfur, which is the second death." (Revelation 21:1-8)

And here we see the matchless beauty for some and the matchless terror for others on the Last Day and the eternity that follows.

How does this move us?

What is our reaction?

What is our *action*?

When you imagine yourself 1,000 years from now, does the thought of sharing paradise with the living Christ lift your soul to unfathomable heights? When you imagine your lost friend, family member, or coworker 1,000 years from now, are you terrified on their behalf and motivated to bring to them the only message that God has supernaturally empowered so that they might be saved?

Our willingness to submit to Him in all things is a direct measure of our walk

THE LIGHT OF SUBMISSION IN A WORLD DARKENED BY REBELLION

"Missions is not the ultimate goal of the church. Worship is. Missions exists because worship doesn't."

John Piper

"Truth by definition is exclusive. If truth were all-inclusive, nothing would be false."

Walter Martin

We are slaves to sin or slaves to Christ. There is no middle ground, however pleasant such imaginary territory might seem to the rebellious mind.

Understanding this is an essential key to Christ-centered worship and Christ-centered living.

It is the author's hope that culturally reimagined terms like "slave", "obedience", and "submission" will come once again to be rightly valued as only being as good or bad as the object to which they are attached. Insofar as this is true – and it always is – then, by any biblically sound and reasonable standard of measurement, there can be no better thing possible for an individual than slavery to Christ, obedience to Christ or submission to Christ. Conversely, we must then understand that there can be no worse condition for an individual than slavery to anti-Christ (which covers all that rejects Him), disobedience to Christ, or rebellion against Christ.

This is the truth that we must live and proclaim. Explicitly.

This is the source and goal of the supernatural Gospel.

This is light.

Our light.

It is Him in and through us.

It is His truth. His liberty. His beauty. His power.

And He has chosen us to bring it to them – all of them; every zombie and God-hater – so that they might be saved.

That is the supernatural calling and power that we have been given.

It is all that we have.

And, by His grace and for His glory, it is all that we need.

ACKNOWLEDGMENTS

The path to producing *Apathetic Christianity* has been made possible, by God's grace, through the presence, prayers and inspiration of many of the most *non*-apathetic Christians that I have been blessed to know personally.

Trina and Jan, to whom this book is dedicated, have been used mightily in ways that I do not have the time to express here. Their passion for truth and persistent pursuit of His call on their lives has been an incredible inspiration, and their friendship has become a most cherished possession.

Jerry Perryman and the rest of Team Reformation back home in the Ozarks are also something of a wonder where example and inspiration are concerned. His grace-seasoned yet determined pursuit of Truth is one supernaturally supercool thing to me.

And to the many new and most inspiringly anti-apathy Christians I've been blessed to connect with since the publication of *Fire Breathing Christians*…you are more of a blessing to me than you will ever know on this side of eternity.

ABOUT THE AUTHOR

Photograph Copyright 2012 Cali Ashton Photography, Nashville, TN

Scott Alan Buss is a wretch saved by grace, a husband to Holly, and father to Rosie and Wolfgang. He and his family make their home in Middle Tennessee, where he is a thankful member of Christ the King Church.

Scott is a writer, speaker, and the founder of R3V Press, where he has published several books. He regularly blogs and podcasts at *Fire Breathing Christian*.

www.FireBreathingChristian.com

THE CURE FOR APATHETIC CHRISTIANITY
ALSO FROM R3VOLUTION PRESS:

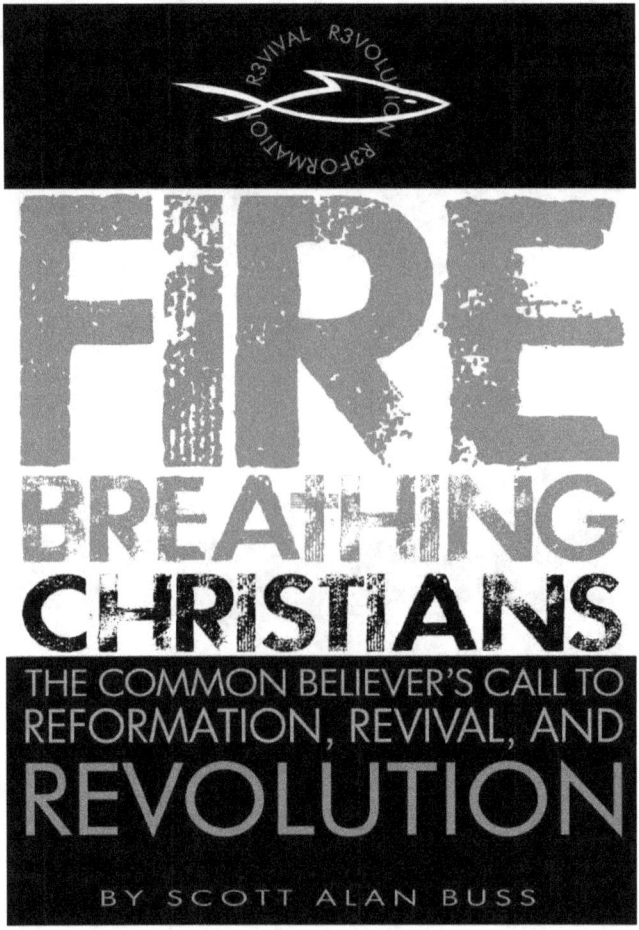

This revised and updated edition of *Fire Breathing Christians* is 416 pages of Christ-centered, Gospel-fueled reformation, revival, and revolution.

www.FireBreathingChristian.com

ALSO FROM SCOTT ALAN BUSS AND R3VOLUTION PRESS:

Fire Breathing Christians – The Common Believer's Call to Reformation, Revival, and Revolution

the beginning of knowledge: Christ as truth in apologetics

Satan's Jackass – The Progressive Party's War on Christianity

Stupid Elephant Tricks – The Other Progressive Party's War on Christianity

On Education - Thoughts on Christ as the Essential Core of Children's Education

the FIRE-BREATHING CHRISTIAN

PODCAST

HELL RAZING RADIO
www.FireBreathingChristian.com

STICK PEOPLE FOR JESUS — A Tale of Two Churches

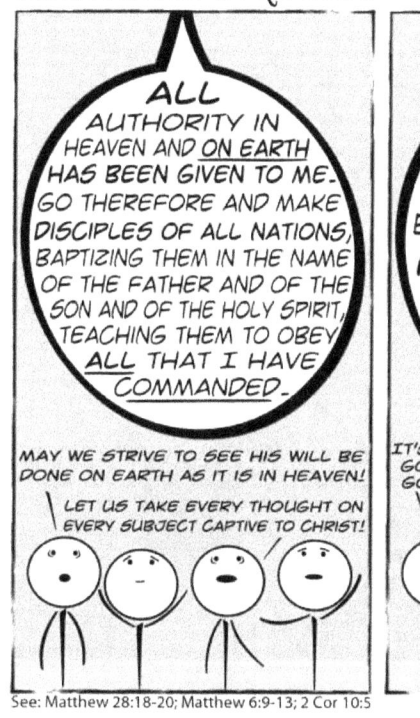

For more *Stick People for Jesus* comics, visit www.FireBreathingChristian.com.

Check out the latest Fire Breathing Tees designs at www.FireBreathingChristian.com

HOME SCHOOL DESIGNS

ALL KNOW GOD DESIGNS

RAZE HELL DESIGNS

BE DANGEROUS DESIGNS

www.ingramcontent.com/pod-product-compliance
Lightning Source LLC
LaVergne TN
LVHW051555070426
835507LV00021B/2590